Rush Shippen Huidekoper

The Cat

A Guide to the Classification and Varieties of Cats and a short Treatise upon their

Care, Diseases, and Treatment

Rush Shippen Huidekoper

The Cat

A Guide to the Classification and Varieties of Cats and a short Treatise upon their Care, Diseases, and Treatment

ISBN/EAN: 9783337177836

Printed in Europe, USA, Canada, Australia, Japan

Cover: Foto ©Andreas Hilbeck / pixelio.de

More available books at **www.hansebooks.com**

THE CAT

A GUIDE TO
THE CLASSIFICATION AND VARIETIES OF CATS
AND A SHORT TREATISE UPON THEIR
CARE, DISEASES, AND TREATMENT

BY

RUSH SHIPPEN HUIDEKOPER, M. D.

VETERINARIAN (ALFORT), ETC.

AUTHOR OF THE AGE OF THE DOMESTICATED ANIMALS,
CONTRACTION OF THE HORSE'S FOOT, IDENTIFICATION OF ANIMALS,
ETC.

WITH OVER THIRTY ILLUSTRATIONS

NEW YORK
D. APPLETON AND COMPANY
1895

TO

JOHN P. HAINES, Esq.,

President of the American Society for the Prevention
of Cruelty to Animals, New York,

in appreciation of his work, which has done so much to increase the care of the home cat and to alleviate the sufferings of the waif, this book is respectfully dedicated

BY

THE AUTHOR.

NEW YORK
PUBLIC
LIBRARY

PREFACE.

WHEN, a month ago, the National Cat Show became an established fact, and inquiries were being made in regard to the classification and qualities of cats, I learned that none of the booksellers in New York had any literature upon the cat except a technical book by St. George Mivart: "The Cat: An Introduction to the Study of Backboned Animals," and the smaller book of Gordon Stables. I determined to prepare the present guide, which I present to the public interested in the useful stable-companion and pretty house-pet. Unfortunately, I was moving my office to the New York College of Veterinary Surgeons at the time, and many of my books, manuscripts, and personal notes were boxed up and have been unavailable for reference. I have drawn freely from the list of books to be found in the Bibliography. The illustrations are drawn mostly from St. George Mivart's book, "The Cat;" from "Our Cats," by Harrison Weir, F.R.H.S.; from Chauveau's "Anatomy" and Raillet's "Zoölogie." I am especially indebted to ARTHUR ERWIN BROWN, Esq., superintendent of the Zoölogical Gardens of Philadelphia, for editing the chapter upon the Zoölogy of the Feline Species; and I am glad to avail myself of this public opportunity of repeating my thanks to him.

RUSH SHIPPEN HUIDEKOPER.

New York College of Veterinary Surgeons,
   154 East Fifty-seventh Street,
      New York, April 16, 1895.

CONTENTS.

CHAPTER I.

                                             PAGE

ZOÖLOGICAL POSITION OF THE CAT FAMILY, WITH A DESCRIPTIVE LIST OF THE VARIOUS FELINE SPECIES 1

CHAPTER II.

AN OUTLINE OF THE ANATOMY OF THE DOMESTIC CAT.................. 21

CHAPTER III.

THE ORIGIN OF THE DOMESTIC CAT AND ITS VARIETIES.

    The Wild Cat.................. 32
    The Egyptian Cat.................. 34

LONG-HAIRED CATS.

    The Angora.................. 40
    The Persian.................. 41

SHORT-HAIRED CATS.

    The Tortoise-shell.................. 46
    The Tortoise-shell-and-White.................. 49
    The Brown Tabby.................. 53
    The Spotted Tabby.................. 56

	PAGE
The Short-haired White Cat	62
Self-colored Cats	65
The Black Cat	65
The Blue Cat	65
The Black-and-White Cat	67
The Siamese Cat	69
The Manx Cat	71

CHAPTER IV.
CARE OF THE CAT.

Housing	75
Feed	78
Breeding	81
Gelded Cats	84
Transportation	85

CHAPTER V.
DISEASES OF THE CAT.

Evidence of Disease	87
Diseases of the Respiratory System.	
Catarrh or Cold	89
Bronchitis	89
Broncho-pneumonia	91
Diseases of the Digestive System.	
Gastritis	93
Constipation and Diarrhœa	95
Jaundice	96
Constitutional Diseases.	
Distemper	99
Glanders	103
Eczema	105
Canker of the Ear	105
Milk-fever	107

Nervous Troubles.
   Convulsions or Fits 108
   Epilepsy 109
Parasitic Diseases.
   Fleas 110
   Mange 111
   Follicular Mange 114
   Stomach Worms 116
   Tapeworm 118
   Ringworm 120
   Trichina 122
   Strongyli 125
Diseases of the Eye.
Diseases of the Teeth.
Diseases of the Claws.
POISONS... 129
ADMINISTRATION OF MEDICINE 131
ANESTHETICS 134
DESTROYING CATS 134

CHAPTER VI.

ETYMOLOGY AND SYNONYMS OF THE CAT 137
EMBLEMATIC SIGNIFICATION OF THE CAT 138

APPENDIX.................................... 141

BIBLIOGRAPHY.

THE COMPARATIVE ANATOMY OF THE DOMESTICATED ANIMALS. By A. Chauveau, M.D., LL.D., etc. (English translation). New York, D. Appleton & Co., 1891.

A MANUAL OF ZOÖLOGY. By Henry Allegne Nicholson, M.D., D.Sc., M.A., etc. New York, D. Appleton & Co., 1883.

ÉLÉMENTS DE ZOÖLOGIE MÉDICALE ET AGRICOLE. Par A. Raillet. Paris, Asselin et Hougeau, 1886.

THE CAT: AN INTRODUCTION TO THE STUDY OF BACK-BONED ANIMALS, ESPECIALLY MAMMALS. By St. George Mivart, Ph.D., F.R.S. With 200 illustrations. New York, Charles Scribner's Sons, 1892.

OUR CATS, AND ALL ABOUT THEM: THEIR VARIETIES, HABITS, AND MANAGEMENT, AND FOR SHOW, ETC. By Harrison Weir, F.R.H.S., President of the National Cat Club. Boston and New York, Houghton, Mifflin & Co., 1889.

THE CAT: ITS NATURAL HISTORY; DOMESTIC VARIETIES; MANAGEMENT, AND TREATMENT. By Philip M. Rule. London, Swan Sonnenschein & Co.

DOMESTIC OR FANCY CATS (illustrated). By John Jennings. London, L. Upcott Gill, 1893.

THE CAT: ITS HISTORY, DISEASES, AND MANAGEMENT. By the Honorable Lady Cust. London, Henry J. Drake.

CATS: THEIR POINTS AND CLASSIFICATION. By W. Gordon Stables, M.D., C.M., R.N. London, Dean & Son.

THE DOMESTIC CAT. By Gordon Stables, M.D., C.M., R.N. London, George Routledge & Sons.

THE CAT

CHAPTER I.

ZOÖLOGICAL POSITION OF THE CAT FAMILY, WITH A DESCRIPTIVE LIST OF THE VARIOUS FELINE SPECIES.

ZOÖLOGICALLY speaking, the cat is a mammal belonging to the order *Carnivora*, or flesh-eaters. Modern classification, based chiefly upon characters drawn from the bony skeleton — which changes slowly with developmental processes through the course of geologic time, and preserves the evidences of common ancestry much longer than the softer parts of the organism — divides the carnivores into three suborders, known as *Cynoidea*, containing the dogs, wolves, foxes, and jackals; *Arctoidea*, including bears, racoons, and most of the so-called fur-bearing animals—otters, weasels, skunks, badgers, etc.; and *Æluroidea*, with four families: *Viverridæ*—the musk-cats or civets and genets, with the paradoxures and ichneumons; *Hyænidæ*—the three species of hyena, with the aardwolf, or *Proteles*, of South Africa; *Cryptoproctidæ*, containing but one savage little member, a native of Madagascar, called "foussa"; and finally the cat's own family, the *Felidæ*.

The degree of perfection reached by any living organism is simply the amount of specialization or adaptation which it has undergone in its relations to the special natural conditions under which its life is passed, and measured by this standard, the cat is the most perfect of carnivores. Feeding upon other animals, which it must pursue with noiseless stealth and capture by an exertion of supreme activity, the cat has padded feet which make no sound in movement; muscles of enormous power and bulk in proportion to its size, and attached to bones addressed to each other at such angles as to form the most complete system of springs and levers for propelling the body known in the whole group; the claws are sharper and curved into strong hooks more than in any other mammal, and by the action of special muscles are withdrawn under the protection of sheathlike pads, that they may escape wear and injury when not in use; no teeth are better fitted for their work—the great canines for tearing, and the scissor-like premolars for shearing off lumps of flesh small enough to swallow; while the short and simple alimentary tract takes up little internal space, and permits of a lithe and slender form suited to the highest activity, at the same time performing its digestive work rapidly, and soon ridding the animal of the burden of the enormous meals which those which feed only when they can are certain to indulge in when the opportunity arises. In the eye, the fibres of the iris, opening to the widest extent, expand the pupil to a full circle, admitting every ray of light which can fall upon it during the darkness of night, and by a rapid and spontaneous contraction—in some species to a narrow slit, in others to a ring as small as a pinhead—shut off all excess of blinding light at midday, and permit minute exactness of vision under either extreme. Add to all these that the coloring of cats is highly assimilated, as it is termed, or suited to concealment among the various shades of ground and foliage among which it lives—as, for instance, the tiger, buffy yellow, with vertical bars of black, is said to blend perfectly with the upright yellow bamboo stems which stand out against the gloomy interspaces of tropical jungles; and the leopard and jaguar, of a similar yellow, with dark spots and rosettes, living largely in trees, are not readily perceived among the mottling of light and shade resulting from the maze of leaves, boughs, and wandering rays of sunlight; while the cats of one color, like the lion and puma, are of neutral shades of gray or yellow, harmonizing well with earth tints on open plains, and inconspicuous under any surroundings. It is thus seen that, with all mammals in the field, none probably is so well armed for the battle of life as is the cat.

This general type of structure is common to all cats, such variations as there are, being only in minor characteristics, but slightly related to their life habits. And psychologically, too, there is quite as much uniformity; all cats are carnivorous, preferring to discover and kill their own prey; all are ferocious and sanguinary; loving retirement; moving with concealment and stealth; never affronting danger, but fighting desperately when injured or when escape is no longer possible. All climb with ease, excepting only the tiger and lion, whose bulk has probably deterred them from acquiring the habit. So persistent are the characters both of body and mind in this family, that in spite of thirty-five centuries or more of domestication, the household tabby to-day preserves far more of its ancestral traits than any other of the four-footed associates of man.

Cats are found all over the world, except in the Australian region, Madagascar, and the West Indies. They are mainly tropical and heat-loving, although a few species range far to the north, as the tiger in Asia and the puma in America. The short-tailed lynxes also predominate in northern regions.

They are naturally a well-marked group, and for the present purpose may be regarded as forming a single genus, *Felis;* the characters upon which most of the genera were based, which various systematists have attempted to set off from the main stem, being uncertain, variable, and hard to specify. Some members of the genus vary greatly in size and color, and we have far from complete knowledge of all the different kinds of cats under nature, but those most commonly recognized at the present time may be briefly recounted:

1. The TIGER (*Felis tigris*). The title of "king of beasts" has long been conferred upon the lion, but by right should be borne by the royal tiger—his superior in beauty, size, and strength. The ingenious observations upon the muscular capacity of animals made by the Rev. Mr. Houghton, at Dublin, showed the strength of the tiger to exceed that of the lion by a full quarter; and on a few occasions when they have been matched together, the tiger has always proved the victor—in modern days as well as in the arenas of Rome.

Tigers are found all through southern Asia, and away to the north in Siberia and Korea, and in the larger islands of the Indian Archipelago, excepting Borneo and Ceylon. Their vertical bars of black and yellow need no description; the sexes are alike, save that the female is somewhat smaller and less powerfully built. A full-grown male should measure about ten and a half feet from tip of nose to end of tail, and in good condition should weigh about four hundred and fifty pounds. Twelve-foot tigers are never seen in life, and owe their existence only to wilful or careless measurement, or more commonly to stretching of the elastic skin when freshly removed. Tigers thrive well in captivity, but do not, as a rule, breed freely. Strange to say, hybrids with the lion are not uncommon in menageries.

2. The LION (*F. leo*) has a very extensive geographical range over the whole of Africa and southern Asia into India, and, as might be expected in encountering such a variety of climates and surroundings, lions from different parts sometimes present marked contrasts in appearance. Some are lighter or darker in color; some males have an enormous growth of long dark hair about the neck and shoulders and on the under side of the body, while in

others it is little more developed than in the female. But these differences are purely individual, and have no specific value. Indeed, Mr. F. C. Selous, the famous hunter and explorer of South Africa, says that in wild lions the mane never reaches the development shown by many specimens in menageries. Young lions are spotted all over the body at birth; the spots usually disappear at from two to three years of age, about the time the mane begins to show, but not infrequently they remain indistinctly on the sides and abdomen throughout life. African lions are usually larger than Asiatic specimens, the male being always the larger, and scaling perhaps four hundred pounds in weight, with an extreme length of ten to ten and a half feet.

3. The LEOPARD (*F. pardus*) covers very much the same countries as the lion, but is more constant in its yellow background of color, covered with rosettes of black spots. It varies greatly, however, in size, some specimens — especially old males — in India reaching a bulk double that of average individuals. Some naturalists and almost all sportsmen erroneously regard

these large examples as a distinct species, which they call the panther. Black leopards are not uncommon, in which the spots show faintly in certain lights, outlined in different degrees of black; these are only what is called melanistic individuals, and make their appearance in the same litter as cubs of ordinary color. Leopards are from five to eight feet long, and are small enough to climb trees without difficulty.

4. The OUNCE (*F. uncia*) is peculiar in that it is rarely found below the snow-line in the Himalayas of India, which it inhabits up to an altitude of eighteen thousand feet; it is also found in central Asia, always at great elevations. It is about the size of the leopard; but as with most inhabitants of cold climates, the fur is long and dense, and the tail is much more bushy than in any other cat, though tigers from Siberia often exhibit these characters as well. The ounce is pale yellowish gray, spotted all over, though the spots show less tendency to form rings or rosettes than in the leopard. The only specimen of this animal which has been brought alive out of its native country was exhibited in the Zoölogical Gardens at London

in 1894. The name "snow-leopard" is often applied to it.

5. The PUMA (*F. concolor*) inhabits all of continental America from Hudson's Bay to the Straits of Magellan—a range more extensive than that of any other cat. It is an adaptable animal, and is equally at home in the canebrakes of the lower Mississippi, the jungle-swamps of Brazil, or at altitudes of twelve thousand feet in the Rocky Mountains. In North America they are usually gray in color, and without spots when adult, though the cubs are spotted like young lions and probably the young of all the one-colored cats. In tropical regions they show a disposition to rufous tints, and skins from South America are sometimes of a rich red tan. This species is known by many vernacular names. "panther," "cougar," "lion," and "mountain-lion" being among them. The latter names appear to have arisen from the fact that the early discoverers of America took the puma to be a female lion—an animal which it resembles in a general way, owing to its uniform color and the absence of a mane.

They are conspicuously secretive, even in this wild and shy family, and in mountainous regions, where their tracks may be daily seen, it is an unusual event to come upon the animal itself. Eight feet in length, including the tail, and one hundred and fifty pounds' weight, would be a large specimen of this species. The head is smaller than in most cats; the muscular system is powerful, and the activity is prodigious.

6. The JAGUAR (*F. onca*) much resembles the leopard. The body-color is of a rather deeper yellow, and sometimes has almost a rosy tinge; the rings formed by the dark spots are, as a rule, larger than in that species, and frequently inclose several irregular marks or spots of the same color. White specimens have been known, and black ones occur as in the leopard. They are heavily built animals, ordinarily about the size of the leopard, but with a slightly shorter tail. Sometimes, however, a large size is reached, Baron Humboldt having seen one as large as an average tiger; and D'Azara, another well-known South American traveler, states that he once knew a jaguar to drag off the body of a horse and swim with it across a wide and deep

river. The species has been known to occur as far north as the Red River in Louisiana; it was formerly not uncommon on the lower Rio Grande in Texas, and ranges far to the south in Uruguay and Argentina.

7. The CLOUDED TIGER (*F. macrocelis*). This fine species, about six and a half feet long, is last in the list of large cats. It inhabits southeastern Asia, with some of the outlying islands. It is of a brownish gray, with darker patches irregularly disposed in vertical markings.

8. The THIBET TIGER-CAT (*F. scripta*), restricted to Thibet, and similar to the last species, but much smaller.

9. FONTANEIR'S CAT (*F. tristis*), pale gray, variously spotted, and marked with rusty brown; found in China.

10. The GOLDEN CAT (*F. moormensis*), about four feet in length, uniform red-bay in color, with a few indistinct spots on the sides. This beautiful species comes from India, where its exact range is not fully made out.

11. The FISHING CAT (*F. viverrina*), a heavily built cat, gray in color, very irregularly marked with dark-brown spots. The body is about

thirty inches in length, and the tail about ten. It is an inhabitant of southern Asia and Ceylon. Alone among cats, it lives upon fish and fresh-water mollusks, which it captures for itself.

12. The BENGALESE CAT (*F. bengalensis*), a very beautiful species from northern India, of a tawny or fulvous gray, with the usual irregular dark markings. Specimens of this and the two preceding species are at present living in the collection of the Zoölogical Society of Philadelphia.

13. The WAGATI (*F. wagati*). This is also a Bengalese cat, yellowish in color, and more or less spotted or striped.

14. The MARBLED TIGER-CAT (*F. marmorata*), a spotted, yellowish-gray cat of medium size, inhabiting Burmah, Malacca, Java, and Borneo.

15. The SERVAL (*F. serval*), a moderately large African cat of rusty or tawny color, with black spots on the body and rings on the short tail, and with very long legs; an inhabitant of the whole of Africa.

16. The GOLDEN-HAIRED CAT (*F. rutila*), a reddish-brown cat with small dark spots, found on the west coast of Africa.

17. The GRAY AFRICAN CAT (*F. neglecta*), a small gray, spotted species inhabiting Gambia.

18. The SERVALINE CAT (*F. servalina*), very similar to the last, but yellowish instead of gray, and found in Sierra Leone.

19. The OCELOT (*F. pardalis*), a beautiful and very variable cat, sometimes gray, often yellow, but always elegantly marked with spots, streaks, and blotches of dark and occasionally brownish gray. Full-grown specimens are sometimes four feet long, and the sexes are similar. The range of the species is about the same as that of the jaguar, but they are more common than the latter in the southwestern United States. These animals are said to be easily tamed, but in the experience of the writer they are usually savage, and less readily domesticated than many other members of the family.

20. The MARGAY (*F. tigrina*), a spotted, grayish cat found in the low woodlands of Central and South America.

21. GEOFFROY'S CAT (*F. guigna*), a small spotted cat of South America.

22. The Ocelot-like Cat (*F. pardinoides*), a small species from Bogota, South America.

23. The Yaguarundi (*F. yaguarundi*). This animal and the succeeding one are remarkably different from most cats in external appearance. The body is long and slender, the legs short, the neck long, and the head elongated and flattened, so that the animal at a first glance has the aspect of a large weasel, rather than one of the *Felidæ*. This species is of a dark gray, sometimes brownish, often almost black, and is of uniform color. The body is less than two feet long, and the tail is of equal length. It is found from the Rio Grande to Brazil.

24. The Eyra (*F. eyra*), similar in form to the last, but usually of a reddish-tan or brownish-yellow color, and considerably larger. Its range is about the same.

25. The Colocollo (*F. colocollo*), a whitish-gray species, about the size of the common cat, with black stripes on the back, sides, and side of the face; an inhabitant of Guiana and northwestern South America.

26. The Rusty-spotted Cat (*F. rubiginosa*), a graceful, pretty little cat of a greenish gray,

sometimes with a rusty tinge, with elongated, sparsely scattered black spots, which give it almost the color of the rich moss-colored bark of a tropical tree; an inhabitant of Ceylon and portions of continental India.

27. The CHINESE CAT (*F. chinensis*), pale yellowish gray, with dark-brown spots, and white on the under surface of the throat and body; an inhabitant of Canton and the island of Formosa.

28. The SMALL CAT (*F. minuta*), much like the Chinese Cat, but smaller and with spots rather more elongated; an inhabitant of the Indian Archipelago.

29. JERDON'S CAT (*F. jerdoni*). This cat is much like the last two species, but has a shorter tail, darker and more distinct spots.

30. The JAVAN CAT (*F. javanensis*), known only from a skin in the British Museum.

31. The BUSHY-TAILED, RED-SPOTTED CAT (*F. euptilura*), about the size of the house-cat; gray; spotted; from Shanghai, China.

32. The SMALL-EARED CAT (*F. microtis*); Mongolia.

33. The LARGE-EARED CAT (*F. megalotis*).

34. The FLAT-HEADED CAT (*F. planiceps*), a

dark-brown cat with silvery tips to the hairs; from Malacca, Sumatra, and Borneo.

35. The BORNEAN BAY CAT (*F. badia*), another unspotted variety.

36. The EGYPTIAN CAT (*F. caligata*). This species varies from a pale yellow to gray, with darkish bands on the legs and toward the end of the tail, and distinct horizontal bands on the sides of the face. This long-tailed cat is probably one of the main sources of origin of the domestic cat.

37. The WILDCAT (*F. catus*) is found throughout Europe and western Asia, although it has become extinct in England. The color is dark gray, banded and spotted, and the tail is comparatively short.

38. The INDIAN WILDCAT (*F. torquata*). This cat much resembles the European Wildcat, but is lighter in color, not so distinctly banded, and more graceful in its form.

39. The COMMON JUNGLE-CAT (*F. chaus*), an inhabitant of India, of moderate size.

40. The ORNATE JUNGLE-CAT (*F. ornata*), from northwestern India; pale brown, with very small spots.

41. The STEPPE CAT (*F. caudatus*), an inhabitant of Bokhara.

42. SHAW'S CAT (*F. shawiana*), from Turkestan.

43. The MANUL (*F. manul*), the beautiful wildcat of Thibet, Mongolia, and Siberia. It is smaller than the common cat, with long, soft hair, yellowish white in color, with some black markings on the legs and body.

44. The STRAW or PAMPAS CAT (*F. pajeros*). This cat represents in South America the Manul of Asia.

45. The NORTHERN LYNX (*F. lyncus*), a moderate-sized cat, with a heavy body, powerful limbs, a very short tail, and sometimes with tufted ears, inhabits the northern portions of Asia, Europe, and America. The relationships existing between these cats are even yet somewhat obscure, but it seems best to regard them all as of one species, of which the Canada lynx and the red lynx, wildcat or catamount, of the United States may be well-marked varieties. The color ranges from gray to reddish brown, always more or less spotted and banded, and much lighter on the under side of the body.

Northern specimens are heavily furred and have very large feet, serving the purpose of snow-shoes during winter. There is much diversity in size, the southern form being smaller than the Canada one, which may reach three feet in length of body, the tail being about five inches. A mounted specimen from northern Europe, in the British Museum, is quite as large as an average leopard. They are extremely shy animals, and in captivity appear to suffer from the publicity which must needs surround them. In fact, they are among the most difficult of all cats to domesticate, and it is rare to see the slightest disposition to become tame.

46. The PARDINE LYNX (*F. pardina*), the lynx of southern Europe.

47. The CARACAL (*F. caracal*). This is a lynx of slender form and very variable color, found from India and central Asia in to Africa.

48. The CHEETAH (*F. jubata*). The skull of this cat is quite different in some details from that typical of *Felis*, and the claws cannot be drawn entirely back into a sheath: the legs are also very long. The species is usually, there-

fore, regarded as forming a distinct genus, *Cynalurus*. The color is yellow, more or less pale, and the whole body is covered with small dark spots. The head is small, the neck somewhat arched, and in full-grown males a short mane is often developed. The long legs give this curious cat somewhat the form of the greyhound. It is of comparatively gentle disposition, and in India, as is well known, is very generally used for hunting or coursing antelope upon the open plains. The animal is a native of India, southwestern Asia, and a large portion of Africa. A not very well characterized species, known as the woolly cheetah, is said to exist in South Africa.

Many other supposed species of cat have been described; but most of them rest upon imperfect and insufficient material, while many of the others may be regarded as individual variations from some of the above better-known forms. With increased knowledge of portions of the earth which at present are little known, others will doubtless be added to the list.

CHAPTER II.

AN OUTLINE OF THE ANATOMY OF THE DOMESTIC CAT.

THE skeleton of the cat differs from that of man and those of the other domestic animals only in trivial details which allow such modification as is needed by the habits of the animal.

Figures 1 and 2 give the outlines of the external conformation of the cat, and the same animal in section, showing the proportionate relations of its skeleton to its exterior as a whole. To any one familiar with the skeletons of other animals it will be seen at once that the thorax or chest, as shown by the curves of the thirteen ribs in Figure 2, is very small in proportion to the body when compared with that of other animals. This means a small lung space, which leaves behind it, however,

Fig. 1.—Exterior of a Cat.

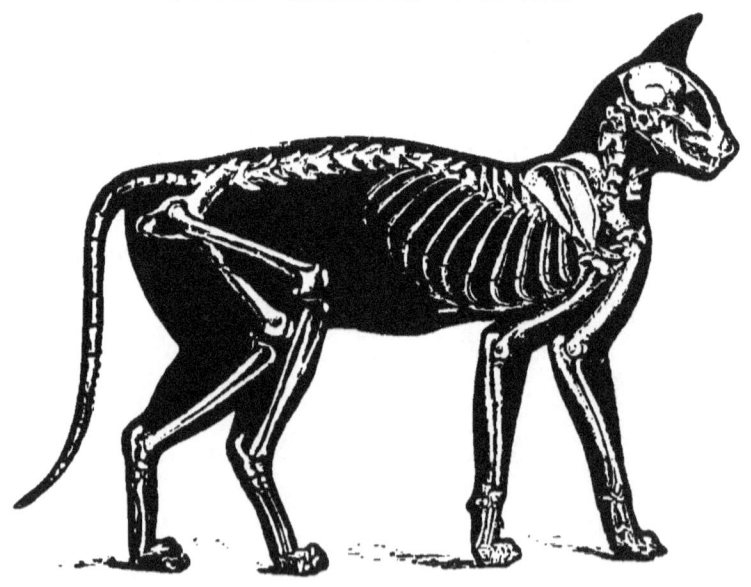

Fig. 2.—Relative Proportion of Skeleton to the Exterior of the Cat.

an immense area for the digestive tract and the organs of propagation. The head is rounded, and the jaws are rather short. The eyes are large, and separated by a considerable interval. The ears become narrow as they ascend, and each stands with its deep concavity directed forward and outward. The neck is a little shorter and less voluminous than the head. The front limbs are shorter than the hind limbs, and consist each of an upper arm, a forearm, and a paw with five short toes. Each hind limb has a thigh, a leg, and a foot with four toes. The proportions of the body are such that both the elbow and knee are placed close to the trunk. It will be seen that the shoulder-blade, the arm, and the forearm lie at very closed angles, as do also the thigh, leg, and foot of the hinder extremities. This conformation indicates at once a character of action of the cat with which we are all familiar. The small lung area allows of quick, active movement, but not of prolonged work. The large space for digestive tract and propagation shows that the animal is capable of taking advantage of all the luxuries of food, with a space for storage, or is, again, able to resist the demands of a long famine. The angular joints of the legs show power and possibility of quick movement, without, however, great speed or extension of stride.

It must be understood here that the enormous jumps which the cat is capable of taking are due to the great power and the closed angles of the joints of its legs; whereas the stride of the animal at a walk, trot, or run is very limited.

Figures 3 and 4 show the skull of the cat and its dentition. It will be seen that the cat's teeth are set at more or less of a hooklike angle, with the points turned toward the inside of the mouth, which gives it a very powerful hold of anything which it grasps. The cat has thirty teeth in all. It will be seen in Figure 4 —which represents the teeth of one side of the jaw—that there is first in front a row of incisors (three on either side—six in all), which are very small, and are practically rudimentary in this animal; then two enormous tush teeth, which enable it to grasp its prey in the shape of the mouse, bird, or a simple piece of meat,

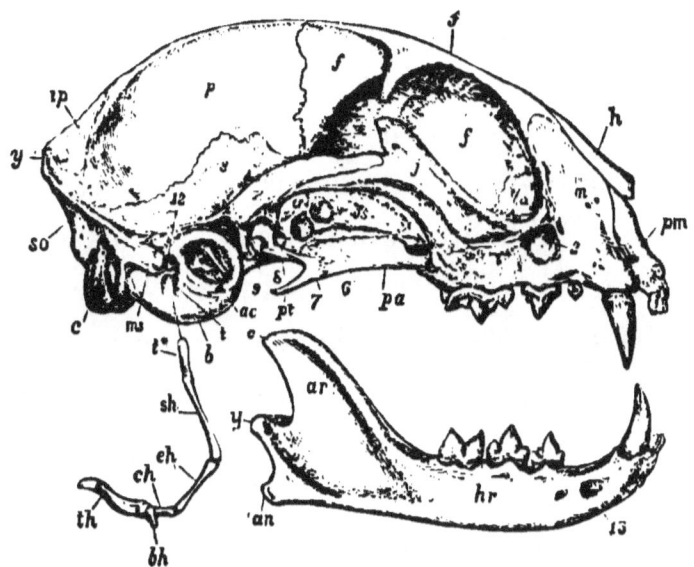

Fig. 3.—Skull of the Cat.

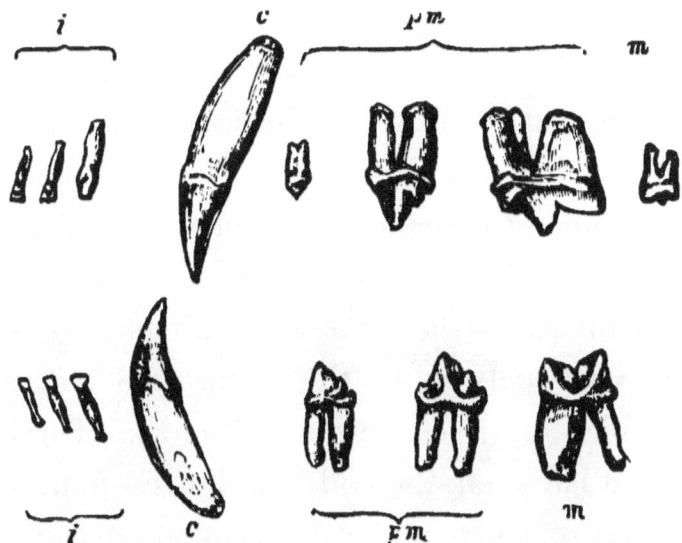

Fig. 4.—Permanent Dentition of the Cat.
i, Incisors; *c*, Canines or tushes; *pm*, Premolars; *m*, Molars.

and hold it firmly; then posterior come the premolars—three in the upper jaw and two in the lower jaw of each side; and behind these the molars—one in each jaw. In the temporary or milk dentition of kittens the molars are absent, leaving but twenty-six teeth. These, it will be seen (Figure 4), have enormous strong roots set in the jaw-bone, while the points are sharp and cutting: which allows of the mangling of any solid food which may be taken, while it does not permit of grinding it, as is necessary in the herbivorous animals, or even, to a certain extent, in the omnivorous animals. The cat, like the dog, after having once grasped its food, tears it to a certain degree, and then swallows it whole, when its powerful stomach and organs of digestion allow of the rapid disintegration of what it may have swallowed.

The muzzle of the cat is soft, with long coarse hairs, ordinarily called the " whiskers" (*vibrissa*), which are really organs of touch. These, like the hairs on the end of a horse's muzzle, or those of most of the domestic animals, are deeply imbedded in the skin, touching at their roots *sensory* nerves, which indicate to the animal, when nosing over foreign objects or when feeling its way in the dark, that its head is coming in contact with foreign bodies; and they are really organs of self-protection. These are seen represented in Figure 5, which also

Fig. 5.—Muzzle of Cat, Showing above, Nose-point and Nostrils covered with Dense Mucous Membrane; at Sides, Vibrissæ; and below, the Lips and Chin.

represents the lips—the upper and lower lip—the nostrils, and the point of the nose. And it will be understood in the description of the various cats in the latter part of this book that when the nose is spoken of as being black or pink, it is meant to indicate that this coloration applies to the mucous membrane surrounding the nostrils, as is seen in the figure, represented by the two dark orifices of the nostrils, surrounded by the grayish hook-lines turning in opposite directions.

The pads of the feet of the cat consist of bulbs of a fibro-elastic, fatty material, covered by an excessively thick and dense epithelial

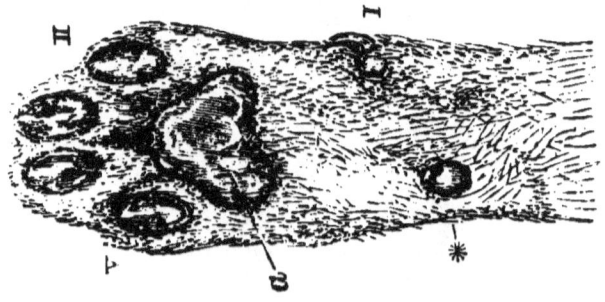

FIG. 6.—RIGHT FOREPAW OF A CAT.

membrane, which is, however, nothing but a modification of the connective tissues and epithelial covering which form the skin of the rest of the body, but is condensed in order to meet the requirements of the extra friction which is demanded of those parts of the feet which come in contact with the ground and must bear the animal's weight. These pads in the forefeet are seven in number, as shown in Figure 6. In the hind feet there are only five. Each pad consists of a mass of fibrous tissue and fat, and a large triobed one is placed beneath the ends of those bones on which the animal rests in walking, as represented in the figure here given.

One essential character of the anatomy of the entire cat tribe consists in the arrangement of the claws at the end of each toe. While the nails of the fingers and toes of man and of the toes of the elephant, the hoofs on the extremity of the legs of the horse, cattle, and such animals, are fixed and practically immovable, and while these same appendages in the claws of the dog and many other animals are fixed, while slightly movable in the softer tissues which imbed them, in the feline species they are excessively movable. In the cat tribe there is in the soft tissue which covers the third phalanx, or the last joint of the toes, a pocket or socket which holds the claw. Under ordinary circumstances, and when the animal is at rest, the claw is drawn back into the socket, and held imbedded there by an elastic ligament, as will be seen in the upper illustration of Figure 7. When, however, an animal of the cat tribe wishes to grasp anything, and use its claws, it flexes the bones of its digital extremities, and tightening the tendon which is seen on the under-surface of both illustrations of

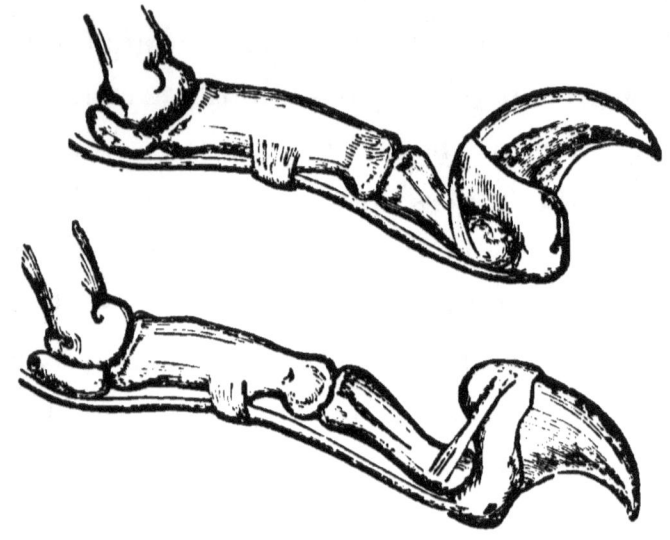

FIG. 7.—UPPER FIGURE: CLAW AT REST, HELD BACK BY ELASTIC LIGAMENT. LOWER FIGURE: CLAW DRAWN DOWN BY CONTRACTION OF TENDON BELOW, ELASTIC LIGAMENT STRETCHED, AND CLAW PROTRUDING.

Figure 7, it draws the claw forward and downward, thereby stretching the elastic ligament. This can readily be verified by taking your own cat at perfect rest, and after patting it gently on the head, pass the hand down over the ends of the toes, when you will find that the claws can scarcely be felt; however, the instant the cat has been wakened and starts to play, or resists the handling it has been subjected to, the claws protrude as the paw and the foot are flexed.

It is not in place here to go into detailed anatomy of the cat. Reference has already been made to the slight development of the respiratory system. The digestive system of the cat is comparatively simple. The stomach is ample, and the intestines which follow it, while convoluted in order to be contained in a limited space, are not subject to the constrictions which are found in the horse and some of the larger domestic animals, and it is rare that we have in the cat troubles coming from obstruction of the digestive tract, unless the animal has by accident swallowed some enormous foreign body.

CHAPTER III.

THE ORIGIN OF THE DOMESTIC CAT AND ITS VARIETIES.

I HAVE referred tersely in Chapter I. to the Wildcat, the Egyptian Cat (which undoubtedly originally was a Wildcat), and the American Wildcat; but I now repeat a description of these, as they are unquestionably the source of origin of the Domestic Cat.

THE WILDCAT (*F. catus*).

While the Wildcat of western Europe is undoubtedly one of the strongest factors in the origin of the ordinary short-haired house-cat of to-day, and the description of it should be original, and that of the house-cat by comparison, the latter is so much more familiar to us all that it is simpler to describe the Wildcat by comparison. The Wildcat differs from the house-cat in being larger and stronger in its body. It has a head which is broader and more heavily boned, and a short, thick tail which does not taper. Its whiskers are more abundant, and the pads of its feet

FIG. 8.—THE WILDCAT.

are, in the males, of a deep black. In color it is a yellowish gray, with a dark longitudinal mark along the back, and it has dark stripes descending more or less vertically on the sides and transversely on the legs. Its tail is ringed with black, and is black at the end. In other words, it is marked much like the domestic Tabby.

The Egyptian Cat (*F. caligata*).

The Egyptian Cat is a native of northern Africa, and was the parent of the cat tamed by the Egyptians, and undoubtedly also one of the originators of our own house-cats. The Egyptian Cat is considerably smaller than the European Wildcat. It is of a yellowish color, darker on the back, and very light on the belly. The stripes on the body are not well marked, though slightly more so on the legs. The tail is slightly ringed.

The American Wildcat (*F. lyncus rufus*).

The American Wildcat is very similar in formation, color, and character to the Wildcat of Europe, but is somewhat stronger and stouter. It undoubtedly has been a factor in the breeding of certain domestic cats in America, but so little so that no importance need be attached to it.

It can now be accepted that the so-called Domestic Cat of to-day is the descendant of certain wild species existing on the several continents ages ago, when the first members were subdued, subjugated, and, by handling, reduced to house-pets, or at least to that semi-domestication which renders them familiar with man, and useful in stables and granaries for the destruction of small vermin, or to be petted in dwellings as companions.

The domestication of the cat took place at a very ancient period. From its small size, and the fact that it is not a choice article of diet, it is not wonderful that we find few or no traces of the smaller varieties of the cat in the dolmens or kokkenmoeddings of Denmark and northern central Europe, nor in the caves of the troglodytes of France, Siberia, and the British Islands. The first evidence of the cat in connection with man is to be found in the ancient monuments of Egypt, Babylon, and Nineveh.

In the Egyptian Gallery of the British Museum is an excellent painting of a tabby-cat, which seems to be aiding a man who is capturing birds. The cat is mentioned in inscriptions as early as 1684 B.C., and it was certainly domesticated in Egypt thirteen hundred years before

Christ. The earliest known representation of the cat as a domestic animal and pet is at Leyden, in a tablet of the Eighteenth or Nineteenth Dynasty, wherein it appears seated under a chair. In Egypt it was an object of religious worship and the venerated inmate of certain temples. The goddess Pasht or Bubastis, the goddess of cats, was, under the Roman empire, represented with a cat's head. A temple at Beni-Hassan, dedicated to her, belongs to the period of Thothmes IV., of the Eighteenth Dynasty, 1500 B.C. Behind this temple are pits containing a multitude of cat mummies. The cat was an emblem of the sun to the Egyptians. Its eyes were supposed to vary in appearance with the course of that luminary, and likewise to undergo a change each lunar month, on which account the animal was also sacred to the moon. Herodotus recounts instances of the strangely exaggerated regard felt for it by the dwellers on the Nile. He tells us that when a cat dies a natural death in a house, the Egyptians shave off their eyebrows; and that when a fire occurs they are more anxious to save their cats than to extinguish the conflagration.

The cat was a common animal, known to the Greeks at the period when Athens represented the civilization of the world; and later, in the Greco-Italian civilization of Herculaneum and Pompeii, in the south of Italy, and in the period of Roman supremacy, it was a well-known animal and the pet of courts and ladies' boudoirs. The first account of its domestication in Great Britain comes at a comparatively late period.

A canon enacted in the year 1127 forbade any abbess or nun to use more costly fur than that of lambs or cats; and the cat was an object of the chase in royal forests, as is shown by a license to hunt it of the date 1239, and by a similar charter given by Richard II. to the abbot of Peterborough.

In résumé, from the foregoing it is evident that the domestication of the cat, or at least its subjugation, which renders it a companion of mankind, took place at a very early period, probably synchronous with the first civilization of man himself. As pussy is an animal which, while savage, wild, and unmanageable in early age and its natural state, is yet small enough to be easily handled, and sensible enough to become reasonably sociable when it has good care and plenty of food, we can readily imagine that even in the earliest of times the young of the Wildcat was caught and brought home to the caves or tents of the first of mankind, to be a companion and pet of the children. Its thrifty, useful habits of mousing and killing vermin made it useful, so that it was probably protected and cared for at a period when mankind first laid up storehouses of grain for winter or future use. I doubt if to-day the cat in the largest city of Europe or the United States is any more of a domestic animal than it was when the nomad Aryan traveled from Asia to the west of Europe.

We have seen from the foregoing that the Domestic Cat probably comes from several sources. The Long-haired Cats derived their origin from the Indian, Bengalese, and various smaller Wildcats of Asia and southern Russia, and are known as the Asiatic, Eastern, or Long-haired Cats.

LONG-HAIRED CATS.

THE ASIATIC OR EASTERN CAT.

The Long-haired Cats, otherwise known as the Asiatic or Eastern Cats, vary only slightly in conformation, but greatly in color and in the quality of their coats. The coat may be woolly in texture, may be coarsish in texture, or it may be as fine as silk; but more commonly there is a mixture of an upper coat of silky hairs with a close, woolly under coat growing around the roots of the former. An important quality in all Long-haired Cats is the frill or "lord mayor's chain," which is a crest of hairs around the neck at the line where the fur of the cheeks pointing downward meets that of the neck pointing forward. They vary in their eyes, ears, and the length and form of the tail. The Long-haired Cats include the various families known as the Angora, the Persian, the Russian, the Chinese, and the Indian.

THE ANGORA.

(Called also Angola.)

The Angora Cat, which has a close relation to the Persian, comes from the province of Angora, in western Asia, which is also well

FIG. 9.—ANGORA.

known for its goats, with fine, silky, long hair, which is used in the manufacture of soft shawls. The Angora has a small head, with a rather short though well-defined nose, more angular than the Persian. The eyes should be large and full, and harmonious in color with the coat of the animal. The ears are rather large, with a tuft of hair at the tip; but they do not look large, as they are imbedded in the long fur which covers the head and neck. The body should be long and graceful, and covered with a long silky hair, finer than that of the Persian, and hanging in tufts and clusters, with a slight tendency to woolliness at the base of the hairs; the legs somewhat short; and the tail long and curving toward the end. The hair on the tail should be long at the base and shorter toward the end of the tail.

The colors of the Angora Cat are varied. The black Angoras and dark slate-colors should have orange eyes; and they, with the blues and the whites, are the most valued, although the light fawns or reds and mottled grays are much esteemed. Mr. Weir says that he does not believe that long-haired Tabbies can be true Angoras.

The Persian Cat.

The Persian Cat differs from the Angora in several essential details. The head is rather larger, with ears less pointed, although these also have tufts of hair at their points. The eyes are large and full. The Persian is larger in the body, and has broader and stronger loins, and from its stronger conformation equals in its activity and strength the graceful form of the more tiger-like Angora. The tail in the Persian is rather longer, turns slightly upward at its tip, and has a greater growth of hair at the end, instead of at the base of the tail as in the Angora. The colors of the Persian are variable; they may be white, black, blue, chinchilla, smoke, and variable degrees of Tortoise-shell and Tabby; but Mr. Weir is again authority for the statement that the Tortoise-shell and the dark-marked Tabby are not Persian Cat colors, but are obtained by crossing with the Short-haired Tortoise-shell and also with the English Tabby. The black is the most valued of colors in the Persian. A good, rich, deep black, with orange-colored eyes and long flowing hair and a heavy mane, constitutes the most perfect form. The next color in value is light slate or blue, which may vary much in its shades from a lilac hue to a deep-blue tone. Then follow the various mixed colors of black and orange, not distinctly blotched enough to be called a Tortoise-

Fig. 10.—A Persian.

shell, nor banded enough to be called a Tabby. The Tortoise-shell and the Tabby are never so well marked in the Long-haired Cats as in the

Short-haired ones, because the longer hairs of the former blend with one another and do not allow so distinct a line of demarcation.

SHORT-HAIRED CATS.

THE EUROPEAN OR WESTERN CAT.

The Short-haired Cat, otherwise known as the European or Western Cat, is the one derived from the European Wildcat, with an intermixture of the blood of the Egyptian Cat. Whatever may have been its original form—which was probably simply a modification of the form of the Wildcat—and its color—which undoubtedly at first was the same as the grayish coat of the Wildcat—it has changed but little except as to a modification of size and a change of color, which is no more odd than the alterations of color of any other animal removed from its natural surroundings and living in civilization. The varieties we make of the Short-haired Cat of to-day are really somewhat arbitrary, and based upon color; but we do find that certain deviations of conformation correspond with certain varieties of color; and it is a fact that by selection of the breeding of like and like, the probability is that the progeny will be like the parent; and yet this is not a fixed fact. We have curious and inexplicable variations of color, especially in the breeding of the cat. One of the most curious of these is exemplified in the Tortoise-shell. It is easy to obtain a beautifully marked female Tortoise-shell; it is difficult to find a good male Tortoise-shell; yet, having found both, and having bred them, while the young females may all turn out good Tortoise-shells, the average male will be a red or yellow Tabby. Careful selection and breeding in cats has been an object of attention only for a comparatively few years. It is but a matter of less than half a century since cat shows have been in vogue, and that much attention has been paid to these animals; and undoubtedly in a few years, when we pay the same attention to the breeding of our cats which we have to that of the thoroughbred horse and all our sporting-dogs, we will obtain more definite and satisfactory results.

The exhibit division and classification of the

varieties of cats—which, as I have just said, is based principally on color—will be found in the Appendix.

It will be seen that in the Prize List of the National Cat Show (*vide* Appendix) the classification of color is not quite so extended; and justly so, as it will require a certain amount of time and more systematic breeding to divide the classes of cats more rigidly. The general divisions will now be given in detail, with a short outline of each variety, and then a résumé of the character or qualities which the animal should present as to the conformation and shape of its head, the color of its eyes, the form and feathering of its ears, the conformation of its body, with the set of the neck and the shape and carriage of the tail, the color and quality of its coat, and the character which is wanted in the appendages of the extremities.

THE TORTOISE-SHELL.

(*Sometimes called Spanish Cats.*)

HEAD.—The head of the Tortoise-shell should be rather small, broad across the forehead and between the eyes, rounded on top, with a nose rather longish, the whole having a somewhat bullety appearance. The head is carried on a rather longish neck, which adds grace, under somewhat savage aspect, to its appearance.

Eyes.—The eyes are round, brilliant, and vary in color from a bright amber to an orange-yellow; the darker the hue the better.

Ears.—The ears are medium in size, rounded at the apex, and broad at the base, giving them an angular form. They should be set well apart and carried well cocked or erect, giving a bright appearance.

Conformation.—The Tortoise-shell is rather a smallish cat; but allowance must be made for the fact that the immense majority of Tortoise-shells are females, which in all the cat families are smaller than the males. The bodies are rather long, giving the animal the graceful turn of the tiger or leopard.

Tail.—The tail is long, thick at the base, tapers toward the end, and has an upward curve. Patches of color on the tail should be as distinct as they are on the body.

Coat—Color and Quality.—The Tortoise-shell in color is black, red, and yellow; the less black the better. The three colors should be distinct, in well-defined patches, with sharp lines of demarcation between them. The color should be rich and deep, and any blur in the

Fig. 11.—Tortoise-shell Cat.

marking or intermixture of the color becomes a weak point in it. The hair should be short, lie close to the body, silken in texture, and have a glossy or brilliant appearance. According to the markings, a Tortoise-shell may be a very homely animal or a most beautiful one. Any white absolutely disqualifies the animal. There is a popular superstition that Tortoise-shells are all females; but this is not the case, for while females are in the majority, males are often to be found, and sometimes are grand, beautiful, large animals.

MERITS.—The Tortoise-shell is one of the best of hunters of all the families of the cat, is a most patient mouser, and is brave to the extreme. It is not over-affectionate, and sometimes even sinister and most ill tempered in its disposition.

THE TORTOISE-SHELL-AND-WHITE.

Another variety of the Tortoise-shell which is frequently seen is one in which there is an intermixture of a certain amount of white, which is usually seen in a blaze on the face, a white breast, and white forelegs and hindlegs, the latter not usually having so much as the former.

HEAD.—The head is small, broad across the forehead and between the eyes. It is round above and depressed toward the lips.

EYES.—The eyes are orange-yellow, full, large, round, and lustrous.

EARS.—The ears are medium in size, narrow and round at the apex, and broad at the base, giving them a conical form. They should be well set and erect.

FORM.—The body is long and narrow, crested by a long, slender, and graceful neck. The shoulders are sloped in harmony with the lithe body, which, with the shortish legs, gives this cat the typical feline gait.

TAIL.—The tail is thicker than that of the Tortoise-shell—especially so at the base—although some Tortoise-shell-and-White Cats have a rather thin tail. The thick tail is, however, preferable. The tail should be marked with black, red, and yellow blotches, and not white.

COAT—COLOR AND QUALITY.—The hair is somewhat coarser than in the pure Tortoise-shell. More white is allowable in the Tortoise-shell-and-White than in the Black-and-White Cat. If the white is entirely distinct, with a clear line of demarcation between it and the black, yellow, and red, as exists between these latter colors, a considerable amount of it is permissible, and adds to the beauty of the animal.

There should be no approach whatever to the Tabby bands or the brownish and grayish color of the Tabby. It is a curious fact that

Fig. 12.—Tortoise-shell-and-White.

the male kittens from the Tortoise-shell-and-White Cat usually come a Red Tabby, or a Red Tabby and White. A good strong blaze on the face, four white feet, a white breast—but the latter not surrounding the neck like a collar—is very popular, and is called "Dutch-rabbit markings." These cats, however, should have good, distinct Tortoise-shell markings over the back and tail.

SIZE AND CONDITION.—The Tortoise-shell-and-White is decidedly larger than the Tortoise-shell in size, and is lithe and elegant in its motion. It is especially beautiful when young, but is apt to become lazy when old—the more so the more white there is in its markings. These cats are excessively cleanly, and vain of their white, spending much of their time in keeping themselves clean.

TABBIES.

The Tabby is one of the commonest of colors, and is found in many breeds of the cat; and still a very well-marked Tabby is comparatively rare. The Tabbies are divided into the Banded Tabbies and the Spotted Tabbies. The name of "Tabby" is derived from "Atab"—a street in Bagdad celebrated for the manufacture of its watered or *moiré* silks, which when sold in England were called "atabi" or "taffety"; and from the similarity of the stripes of the banded and the brindle cats, the latter were called "Tabby." Weir says that in the south of England (Norfolk and Suffolk) the Tabby is called a Cyprus Cat; and he found in Bailey's Dictionary (1730 A.D.) that "Cyprus" was a kind of cloth made of silk and hair, showing wavy lines on it, and coming from Cyprus. Evidently, therefore, the "Taffeta" or "Tabby" indicates the striping, and not the color.

The Tabby presents numerous varieties in color and shade, but may be divided into four general classes:

1. The Brown Tabby.
2. The Spotted Tabby.
3. The Blue or Silver Tabby.
4. The Red Tabby.

The Brown Tabby.

The Brown Tabby has a ground color of a rich, reddish dark brown, with no white, and even, regular bars and bands of solid, shining black over the face, head, breast, sides, back, belly, legs, and tail. The face, legs, breast, and belly should have more of a rich red orange tint than the back. The bands should be graceful in curve, distinct, and

Fig. 13.—A Well-marked Tabby.

clearly defined, so that there is a perfect demarcation in the line between the black and the brown, and not mixed and blurred. The Banded Tabby should not be spotted in any way, beyond a few spots which almost always

Fig. 14.—BADLY MARKED TABBY (BANDS TOO BROAD).

occur on the face and sometimes on the forelegs. "The clearer, redder, and brighter the brown the better."

HEAD.—Not too large; not too wide; rather longer than broad.

NOSE.—Deep red, bordered with black.

EYES.—Orange, slightly greenish in shade.

EARS.—Medium.

LEGS.—Rather long, for grace of action.

BODY.—Long and narrow, with deep chest.

TAIL.—Long and tapering.

FEET.—Black; black pads and claws, yellowish white around.

Black lips and brown whiskers are allowable, but orange-tinted are far preferable, and pure white should disqualify.

A *Brown* Tabby should be *orange-brown*. The dark brownish-gray Tabbies are simply ordinary Tabbies.

The Spotted Tabby.

The Spotted Tabby may have any base color which is common to the cat. This base color may be brown, red, or yellow; but whichever color it is, it must be spotted with black. There should be no bands whatever, for when these exist it makes a poorly marked Banded Tabby. What were lines in the Banded Tabby should be interrupted regularly, leaving black spots, which in a well-marked Spotted Tabby appear in lines, straight, or with grace-

Fig. 15.—A Spotted Tabby.

ful curves in the neighborhood of the neck and shoulders, but always interrupted into spots. The spots should be medium in size, and the better and more distinctly defined they are the better the Tabby. If spots exist on the face they are especially valuable. There should be no white. The general conformation given for the Banded Tabbies applies to the Spotted Tabby; but the nose should be dark red, and the eyes a yellow-orange; the less greenish the better.

In the Brown Spotted Tabby the pads of the feet are always black, and in the Yellow or Red Spotted Tabby they may be pink. (The spots should not be annulated.) The Spotted Tabby is usually a very large cat, a great mouser and hunter, a brave animal, well capable of taking care of itself against other cats and dogs, and approaches in its general characteristics in many ways to the Wildcat.

The Blue or Silver Tabby.

HEAD.—Its head is small and broad, with a long, sharp nose.

EYES.—The eyes are orange for the Blue

Tabby, yellow for the Silver Tabby, and for both should be large, piercingly bright, and lustrous.

Fig. 16.—A Good Silver Tabby.

Ears.—The ears are medium or somewhat longish.

Form.—In form these cats have long, narrow, graceful bodies, with long neck and excessively graceful general contour.

Tail.—The tail is long, thick at the base, curves upward, and should have rings.

Coat—Color and Quality.—The hair should be short, even, smooth, and silky. The base color should be a distinct blue or a silver-gray striped with black. In the Blue the color should be a rich, deep, bright blue; in the Silver very much lighter, but of a very bright color. The black bands should be jet-black, and narrow, clear, and sharply defined. The cushions of the feet are always black. The Blue or Silver Tabby is usually a much smaller animal than the Brown Tabby.

The Red Tabby.

Head.—The head is smallish, with the nose long and tapering.

Eyes.—The eyes may be orange-colored or yellow in color, but should be deep-set, full, round, and lustrous. A beautiful rich yellow is perhaps the preferable eye.

Ears.—The ears are medium in length.

Form.—The form should be long, narrow, and graceful, like the Silver Tabby, and, like it, it should have a long tail, thick at the base, curved upward, and surrounded with rings.

COAT — COLOR AND QUALITY. — This cat should have short, even, smooth silky hairs like the Blue Tabby. The color should be of a deep, rich, reddish brown, bright red, or yellow. The belly and inside of the legs are of a brighter color; the ears and the nose of a deeper color. The bands are formed of a much darker red, which, however, should be as distinct from the lighter base color of the animal as possible; and the rings should be especially well marked around the throat and chest. The Red Tabby should have no white whatever. In size it corresponds much to the Brown Tabby.

This cat is an important factor in breeding Tortoise-shells. In fact, many of the male kittens in the litter of a Tortoise-shell are Red Tabbies, while the females are Tortoise-shells.

They are good-natured domestic cats, great mousers, and hunters for birds, as they climb well; and they are also expert fishers.

White Cats—Short-Haired.

HEAD.—The heads of White Cats are rather small, and round above. The forehead is broad across and broad between the eyes. The nose is rather longish.

EYES.—The eyes should be blue—that beautiful soft blue of a good turquoise, or the sky-blue of a perfect, clear day. Yellow eyes, however, are permissible; but the yellow should be a clear, rich yellow. Greenish eyes are a serious defect. The eyes should be large, round, full, and soft in their appearance, and should be of the same color. Eyes of a different color are not allowable, though these we sometimes find—one blue and the other yellow, or one green with the other of either color.

EARS.—The ears are medium in size, narrow and round at the apex, and broad at the base, and are feathered on the inside.

FORM.—The White Cat has a long, narrow body, with a long, slender, graceful neck. It has a shoulder well sloped, and legs of medium length, slender and delicate, with small round feet.

TAIL.—The tail should be long, thick at the base, and tapering toward the end. It should be carried low, almost trailing on the ground.

COAT—COLOR AND QUALITY.—The White

FIG. 17.—WHITE SHORT-HAIRED CAT.

Cat should have a very short coat, even in length, and lying close to the body; it should be of a silky texture and glossy appearance. The most choice color is a delicate yellowish white—sometimes a slightly bluish white. The gray-white is a decidedly inferior color. A long coat on a White Cat indicates some intermixture with the Angora. White Cats are seldom of great size, and they have graceful, easy movements, but are not languid. The White Cat is of a timid disposition, very fond of petting and cuddling; it is quiet in its manners, delicate in its temperament, and honest in its character. It would much prefer to be fed from the saucer, and from the table while lying on a chair, than to go roaming for prey or stealing from the kitchen. White Cats are, however, sometimes excellent mousers, and are especial pets with millers, as their color can scarcely be seen among the sacks of flour. White Cats are very often deaf, and sometimes blind, without any appearance of organic change in the eyes.

The Albino, which is a white cat with pink eyes—due to an absence of pigment in the iris—must not be included in the group of White Cats, as it may come from any breed, when the absence of color is due to a physiological aberration during development.

Self-colored Cats.

The Self-colored Cats are those which are entirely of one solid color, which may vary in its hue or tint, but must not have any intermixture of white or of any other color. The Self-colored Cats are the Black, the Blue, the Red, and the Yellow. Whatever the color, it should be distinctive and of a rich lustre. The black should be a jet, shining black, the blue of a rich slate or true blue, and the red and yellow of rich colors. The description of the Blue Cat for conformation will suffice for all of the Self-colors.

The Blue Cat.

The Blue Cat is called the "Maltese" in America. This cat has been known under various names in England. It was first shown as the "Archangel Cat," then called the "Russian Cat," also the "Spanish Blue" and "Chartreuse Blue," and recently has been called the "American Blue." This latter name is probably due to the fact that the Maltese for some years has been a very favorite cat in America, and has probably been bred more carefully than any other breed of cat, so that its representatives formed a distinctive type of good quality.

HEAD.—The head should be small, broad at the forehead and between the eyes, rounded

FIG. 18.—BLUE CAT.

above, and tapering to the lips below. The nose should be long, and the end of it black.

EYES.—The eyes should be:
>Orange-yellow for the Blue Cat;
>Orange for the Black Cat;
>Yellow for the Gray Cat;
>Gold for the Red Cat.

EARS.—The ears are medium in length, somewhat pointed.

FORM.—The Self-colored Cats should have a narrow, long body, lithe in appearance, with a long and graceful neck on which the head is well poised. The legs are medium in length, with small round feet.

COAT—COLOR AND QUALITY.—The coat should be short, with hairs of even length lying closely to the body, and silky and glossy, with a rich lustre of whatever the color of the animal may be. The Blue should be a rich light blue; and it is decidedly preferable in all the Self-colors that the tint should be perfectly even over the whole body, and not shade off into a lighter one.

BLACK-AND-WHITE CATS.

The Black-and-White Cat should have the same general conformation, head, set of ears, and carriage of tail as has already been given for the Tabbies.

EYES.—The eyes vary somewhat from an orange-yellow to a green, or that rich green called "sea-green."

COAT—COLOR AND QUALITY.—The black of

the top of the head, body, and tail should be a dense, bright, rich black, and the white markings should be distinctive. It has a white nose running somewhat to a point between the eyes, and the white extends down the throat,

Fig. 19.—Black-and-White Cat.

forming a shield on the breast. There should be no black on the lips. The feet are white, as are the pads underneath them. There should be a perfectly clear, distinctly curved outline at the point of juncture of the two colors. The coat should be thick, silky, and glossy. Sometimes it is slightly ticked with white, which, if it occurs evenly, is not a serious blemish. Black-and-White Cats are usually large, with stout legs, and the ankles of the white ones somewhat close, which gives them great power of movement. According to the care which the Black-and-White Cat receives, it tends more than any other cat to become fat and indolent, or ragged and wretched, as the case may be. The Black-and-White Cat is affectionate and cleanly, but is a selfish animal, and is not one for children to play with.

The Royal Cat of Siam.

The Royal Cat of Siam is an odd but rather attractive cat, from its graceful form, and from the peculiar, strikingly marked black head, tail, and extremities.

HEAD.—The head is small and broad at the eyes, but narrows above at the forehead. The nose is long and broad, the cheeks narrow, and the lips full, giving a sort of square appearance to it.

EYES.—The eyes are almond-shaped, placed

at an angle in the head, reminding one exactly of those of the Chinese or other Mongolians of the human race. They are of a rich opalesque blue, but appear reddish at dusk and at night.

Ears.— The ears are large and wide, with few hairs on the inside.

Fig. 20.—Royal Cat of Siam.

Tail.— The tail is short and thin, but should be perfectly regular and have no break or kink in it.

Coat— Color and Quality.—The coat is short, somewhat woolly, but soft and silky. The preferable colors are a dun or fawn color, although they are sometimes a silver-gray or a light orange. The entire mask of the face and ears and the legs and tail are black. The Royal Cat of Siam is a small animal, narrow in the body, lithe and graceful. The legs are thin and short. The neck is long and small, and the feet are long.

The Manx Cat.

The Manx Cat differs from the ordinary cat only in being tailless, or nearly so, the most choice families not having any tail at all. If they have a short rudimentary tail it should be boneless; but sometimes they have short, thin, twisted tails, or tails in the shape of a knob. Some Manx Cats, however, have very long tails, even ten inches in length. The hind legs are proportionately longer and somewhat heavy, which gives the cat when running or jumping somewhat of the action of a rabbit; but this is more imaginary than real, and the supposed similarity is due rather to the character of the tail. Most Manx Cats are rather smallish, with a head small for their size, set on a thick and long neck. The eyes are large, round, and full. The ears are medium-sized, rounded at the apex, and hairless within. The Manx Cat varies in color, running to Tabbies and all the mixed colors. A white Manx Cat

Fig. 21.—Manx Cat.

is practically unknown, and black ones are excessively rare. The Manx Cat really can be classed as a monstrosity, having been developed probably by the interbreeding of some freak of nature in the form of a cat which inhabited the Island of Man at an early period.

An ordinary cat can easily be rendered tailless if operated on at a young age; and as this is often done, especial attention should be paid to see that the absent tail is natural and that there is no scar as evidence of operative interference, or, as such things are called in dog shows, "faking."

CHAPTER IV.

CARE OF THE CAT.

THE care of the cat is of very much more importance in the close surroundings of city life than it is in the country, where the animal has as much freedom as the barefooted, half-dressed boy who can be trusted to run the farm over, and is supposed to be safe whether rooting in the garden of vegetables, sunflowers, and hollyhocks, playing in the calf-pen, or investigating the poultry or pigs. In the country the cat has the opportunity of finding mice, birds, and its feral prey, and can always fall back on a goodly feed from the milk-pan of the dairy and the rear of the kitchen. It breeds as it pleases, and demands little care or attention beyond the interest the children or housewife take in the kittens which appear from some corner, after they are able to run themselves, and meet a fate of selection, when the one or two are to be kept and the rest to be drowned.

In the city and large towns it is different. The cat in the environment of civilization must be fed, looked after, and guarded in its moments of freedom; and a guide to the care of the cat applies rather to city cats than country ones, except such portions as are needful for the finer-bred cats, which require special care at all times.

In towns the cat should wear a collar on which the name of the owner is engraved; although there is the serious objection to a collar that it breaks the hairs and marks the neck. In New York the Society for the Prevention of Cruelty to Animals is empowered with a most satisfactory law for the protection of cats and is most liberal in its care of them (*vide* Appendix).

Housing.

The cat is an excessively cleanly animal, and when housed should be provided with means for remaining so. A small box, or—

what is better, as it can be well washed—a galvanized flat pan such as is used for roasting meat, should be placed in some well-ventilated corner out of sight, and kept filled about an inch deep with sand, clean earth, or sawdust. Perhaps the latter is preferable, as it can be burned. The litter should be changed frequently.[1]

There should be in some convenient corner —near the window, in order to get sunlight if possible, at the same time not in a draft—a basket kept filled with clean oat straw or with flannel. While a flannel cushion looks the prettier, clean oat straw, in which the cat can turn and roll, allows it to keep its coat much cleaner and in better order; but the straw, of course, has the disadvantage of getting scattered over the floor when the animal leaves its basket. Wherever it is possible, the basket should be in the sunlight, as cats love to bask. The basket and its filling must be kept abso-

---

[1] For an extended and complete description of the housing of cats on a large scale—"catteries" or "cat-runs"—see "Domestic and Fancy Cats," by John Jennings.

lutely clean. If the animals are at all troubled with fleas or other insects, the bedding can be sprinkled with a little flowers of sulphur, which will drive them off.

In cleaning the cat never use a comb; it breaks the hairs and renders the coat rough. Brush the coat well with a soft brush, or with a mitten which is known as a bath-mitten. The coat of the cat can be improved very materially by washing; but this is difficult unless the animal is very tame, and even then can only be well done by its absolute owner or an attendant of whom it is fond. To wash a cat, make a soft soap-sud, comparatively thick; apply commencing at the hind quarters and tail, and gradually rub in until the ears are reached. After the soap-suds have been thoroughly rubbed in, dip the animal, hind feet first, into a tub of tepid water, when it can be gently patted over with the hand, and then dipped into another tub of tepid water, to rinse it off. The animal should then be wrapped up in a soft bath-towel and the excess of water pressed out; and it should then be put into a basket of clean oat straw and kept in a warm place, where it will finish the drying and cleaning for itself by rolling in the straw and by licking itself, after which it can be brushed with a soft brush.

For a simpler form of dressing to make the coat shiny, the animal can be sponged over with a very little perfectly fresh olive or cocoanut oil, or with a little perfectly fresh cream, which is then wiped off with a sponge slightly damped, or with a towel, and the animal put into the basket of oat straw to clean itself.

FEED.

In the country, or in a small house where the cat has full freedom of the kitchen and back yard, very little attention is required in regard to feeding, as the animal will pick up from the scraps the very diet which it is best for it to have. When cats, however, are kept in closer confinement, and in city houses, more attention must be paid to their food; for inattention to this is the principal cause of most of the maladies with which they are affected. In the first place, the dishes from which a cat is fed must be absolutely and immaculately clean, and at each fresh feed should be scalded before they are used again. Milk is not only the traditional diet of the cat, but also forms one of the principal articles of food for it. The milk should be perfectly fresh, as sour milk is apt to produce digestive troubles, especially diarrhœa. Sour milk, however, is useful sometimes as an adjunct in the treatment of worms. While the cat drinks a considerable quantity of milk, it prefers water when it is really thirsty, although it takes only a very small quantity of this. The water, like the milk, should be in an absolutely clean pan. There is a very useful pan — which can be found in porcelain at the china-shops, or can be readily made by a tinner — consisting of a pan divided in the center by a partition, in which the milk is placed at one side and the fresh water at the other; this insures that the water is emptied out each time the milk is replaced, in order to clean the pan and allow it to be perfectly fresh. Bread (preferably stale bread) and the ordinary crackers, water biscuit, or oatmeal biscuit, can be added to the milk. Spratt's Patent has a cake for cats which is very useful for occasional diet. Oatmeal porridge forms an excellent diet, and vegetables should be given from time to time. Most cats are very fond of asparagus and celery, but will at times eat almost any vegetable. In cases of diarrhœa or looseness a little boiled rice is a good addition to the milk. There seems to be a prejudice on the part of some people against the feeding of meat to cats, which is unwarranted; and a cat is better for an occasional feed of meat — even once a day in small quantities. They much prefer it raw, and prefer mutton to beef. The traditional cat-meat of the "cat-meat man," which is known so well in England, is made of horse-flesh, and is a wholesome, good food; but the marketing of that is practically unknown in America. Fish is a very favorite diet with the cat, and can be given from time to time; but the fish should be perfectly fresh, as all meat ought to be, for putrid meat is much more apt to produce digestive troubles in cats than it does in the other carnivora; in addition to which, its use by the animal gives it an offensive odor in the house. In résumé, the diet of the cat, with a basis of sweet, fresh milk, can be made up of any of the foregoing articles, if care is only taken to insure the absolute cleanliness of the pans from which the animal is fed, the good condition of the food itself, and that the diet shall be varied. Often when a cat has been kept on one diet steadily for some time it loses its appetite, and appears dumpish, or even ill, when a simple change of food will bring it back to itself at once. Boiled liver is useful once in a week or ten days, or when the cat is a little off its feed, as it acts as a laxative. It is not, however, good diet for regular use.

Breeding.

The period of gestation in the cat varies from fifty-six to sixty-three days. The cat will breed some three or four times in the year, and has a variable number in each litter of its kittens — sometimes two or three only, and sometimes five or six. A young cat is apt to have but two or three at its first pregnancies, and when it reaches the age of four or five years it has a larger number, which diminishes again as the mother becomes older. Long-haired and more highly cultivated cats have smaller litters than the common Tabby which has the run of the barn and stable.

The Wildcat breeds twice a year, and has a somewhat longer period of gestation—about sixty-eight days.

A female cat, or the "queen" cat, as she is called, is usually ready for her first pregnancy at six months of age; but it is not advisable to breed her before she is nine months to one year of age, as at the earlier period she has not attained her growth, and pregnancy is apt to stunt her in size.

The stud cat should not be used until he is one or perhaps two years of age; and he should be in perfect condition of health, with a good coat on him, when given service. When the queen cat gets ready for service she gives unmistakable evidence of it by her peculiar meows and in other ways which are familiar to every one. She should be immediately shut up in a room or loft where she is inaccessible to any cat but the stud who has been chosen for her. The period in the "queen" lasts for some four to ten days; but to be absolutely safe it would be well to extend the confinement to twelve days. The tom-cat who has been selected for her can be placed in the room with her for a period of twenty-four hours, extending from one day over the night until the next day, which is quite as satisfactory as if he remained with her for a longer period. The queen cat usually becomes sterile at about the age of nine years; but Jennings gives an example where a cat had kittens in her nineteenth year.

The average life of a cat which has been well taken care of, and has not met with accident, is from twelve to fifteen years. The oldest cat whose age is authentically known is given to be twenty-four years.

The kittens are born blind and deaf and almost absolutely helpless. At the end of about nine days their eyes begin to open and they are able to use their legs, when they are first seen by the public and fit to be handled. They can be weaned at the end of the third week, but it is preferable to allow them to remain with the mother for a longer time. If any of the kittens are to be destroyed or removed from the mother, the whole litter should not be taken at once, but the young ones should be removed one or two at a time, which leaves the others to gradually diminish the milk-supply of the mother. If the whole litter is removed at once the mother is very liable to be affected with milk-fever—a severe fever, with local inflammation of the mammary glands, which may destroy them for future use.

Kittens lose their temporary or milk teeth and acquire their full dentition of permanent teeth at between five and seven months of age; so that if a kitten has its entire permanent dentition, with the teeth completely out of the gums, it can be assumed to be over six months of age, and is to be regarded as such by the judge at cat shows.

Gelded Cats.

The operation of rendering the cat neuter is comparatively common, and has many advantages for some classes of cats; the cats grow larger and lose the strong odors which are sometimes offensive in the tom-cat around an apartment, and the cats become home bodies, not having the temptation of "toms" to wander into the world. The gelded cat is quite as good a mouser and is as brave as any other cat, although it is apt to become fat and lazy if not forced to a certain amount of exercise. The operation is usually done at about six months of age, but if done properly can be done on a cat of any age. Female cats are sometimes operated upon, but in these the operation is attended with considerable danger.

Transportation.

In carrying the cat from one location to another, or in sending it to and from shows, the greatest care must be used to see that the case in which the animal is carried is sufficiently strong to resist injury from other boxes or articles of luggage, and that it is provided with proper air-holes to insure perfect and free ventilation. It should be lined, so that the animal will not injure its coat on any rough or jagged surface, or on the heads of nails or screws which have been carelessly left in it. The author has a basket, purchased in Paris, in the form of a good-sized hand-bag, built with a floor, ends, rear, and top, quite strong enough to prevent breaking, although it is very light. This is covered with leather to represent a traveling-bag. The front has a wire screen which can be dropped and buckled, and this is covered by a loose flap of leather similar to the rest of the case, which can also be buckled down. When closed, ample entrance of air is left for ventilation, and the bag has exactly the appearance of an ordinary traveling-bag. When in a railroad-car or elsewhere, the leather flap can be lifted up, leaving the cat secure, but at the same time allowing it to see its owner or be amused with surrounding objects.

CHAPTER V.

DISEASES OF CATS.

EVIDENCE OF DISEASE.

WHENEVER a cat becomes ill from any disease which is more than trivial, whether it be a fever, an inflammation of one of the organs, or an injury which is somewhat serious, it shows that it is ill more decidedly than any other animal. It appears more sick with troubles of the same severity than do other animals. With the commencing illness the cat loses its appetite, and seeks a dark corner, where it wants to remain out of sight. The nose becomes hot, there is inappetence or total loss of appetite, the coat becomes dry and harsh, and the animal lies quiet, sleeping most of the time, unless there is any degree of pain, when it gives evidence of it by constant crying. At the first symptoms of digestive troubles, and even in fevers and other troubles, if the cat can reach a grass-plot it immediately eats a quantity of grass, which it swallows and retains until the stomach is irritated, producing vomiting, and acting as a laxative to the intestines. This can be considered a natural febrifuge, just as one would give a child or a person a little nitre or a small dose of Rochelle salts at the commencement of an illness. At this time it is well to give cats a small dose of Glauber's salts or of castor-oil, exactly as one would do for a child, or to place a half-teaspoonful of bicarbonate of soda or flowers of sulphur in a saucer of milk, and put it with the cat in a quiet, darkened room.

The diseases of cats, like those of other animals, are divided into diseases of the respiratory system, which include colds, catarrh, bronchial troubles and other diseases of the lungs; diseases of the digestive system, including those of the stomach, the intestines, and the liver; constitutional diseases, such as fevers, infectious distemper, glanders, and eczema; parasitic diseases, such as fleas, mange, and worms; nervous troubles; and local diseases of the eyes, teeth, and claws.

Diseases of the Respiratory System.

Catarrh or Cold.

A cat may take cold in the head just as a baby might do, with inflammation of the mucous membrane lining the nose, the pharynx or larynx. The symptoms are a discharge from the nostrils, more or less difficulty of breathing, due to the obstruction of the nostrils, which are filled with matter, and choking of the throat, due either to the inflammatory condition of it or to the discharge accumulating in the throat. In the former case pressure on the throat will produce a spasmodic cough, and show that there is a tenderness of this organ. Simple catarrh is attended with but little fever or constitutional disturbances.

Bronchitis.

Bronchitis is an inflammation of the tubes leading from the lungs to the exterior. In this the cough is more violent; there is a discharge from the nose and throat, but the amount of phlegm is increased after an attack of coughing. By auscultation, or examining the chest-sounds by the ear, mucous râles can be heard as the air passes through the matter which partially fills the bronchi.

Simple colds and bronchitis do not require much treatment. The cat should be placed in a quiet, darkened corner, and be protected from drafts. It should not have food forced upon it, although it should have a small saucer of water, in which can be placed a little bicarbonate of soda or flowers of sulphur, and a small saucer of fresh milk, which it can take if it wants. It is better to place only a small quantity of milk at a time, as the owner can then judge how much the cat is taking, and there is no chance of the milk souring. If there seems much fever, a drop or two of aconite can be placed in two tablespoonsful of water in the saucer, and renewed when the water is finished. If there is much inflammation of the throat, a dose can be given every few hours of one grain of quinine, two drops of fluid extract of belladonna, and five drops of syrup of squills, in a teaspoonful of sweetened water; and the throat and sides of the body can be rubbed with camphorated oil.

Broncho-pneumonia.

Broncho-pneumonia is the ordinary form of pneumonia in the cat. It may occur primarily after exposure to cold, or it may be the secondary result of a bronchitis which has lasted for some little time. The pneumonia in the cat, like that in the dog, is a broncho-pneumonia, or a pneumonia due to filling up of isolated little lobules in the lung of the animal, and differs from the ordinary pneumonia of man and the horse, in which latter the inflammation invades a whole lobe of the lung. In broncho-pneumonia there is more fever than in simple bronchitis. The constitutional symptoms and debility of the animal are more marked, with usually a total loss of appetite. On auscultation, in addition to the mucous râles which are heard in bronchitis, we have "sibilant" râles, or sounds of more or less sharpness, like those of a whistle, which are due to the hepatization or filled-up lobules pressing upon and compressing the lumen of the air-tubes which lead to lobules of sound lung-tissue. Broncho-pneumonia in the cat may also be caused by the presence of parasites lodged in the lung-tissue and an irritation producing an effusion and filling the air spaces. (*Vide* Parasites, Figure 30, p. 125.) This form of broncho-pneumonia at the outset resembles in its symptoms an ordinary broncho-pneumonia, but is to be diagnosed later, either by the detection of the parasite in the discharge which the animal coughs up, or by the fact that the broncho-pneumonia does not run its regular course, but gets better in a few days, or gets decidedly worse, with more lung-tissue filling up; and that it assumes a chronic form, with the local symptoms of sibilant râles to be heard, unchanged in size and location, accompanied by the absence of the severe constitutional symptoms.

One finds in certain books a description of consumption of the cat. If by consumption the authors mean tuberculosis (which the word technically does), they are absolutely in error; for tuberculosis is almost an unknown disease in the cat, and even by inoculation can only be produced in animals which have been rendered lymphatic by a prolonged close confinement.

In the commencement of broncho-pneumonia the same treatment can be used as for colds and bronchitis. If the disease continues it is well to give, in addition, thirty drops of whisky or brandy in a spoonful of water several times in the day. Should the animal become very much debilitated and absolutely refuse to eat, it can be given a teaspoonful of a mixture of the yellow of one egg beaten up, four tablespoonsful of milk, and two teaspoonsful of whisky every few hours; but it is not advisable to force food on it except in extreme cases. In addition to the milk which is kept at the side of the cat, it can be tempted from time to time with a small bit of raw beef pounded into a pulp, and with a small saucer of the juice of the beef, or of the pure beef-juice as it runs from a cut of roast beef.

Diseases of the Digestive System.

Gastritis.

Gastritis, or inflammation of the stomach, is produced by overfeeding and too frequent feeding, or feeding with irritating food, or by the ingestion of foreign bodies or poison in the stomach. It may also be secondary to constitutional diseases.

The symptoms of gastritis are vomiting, first of the contents of the stomach, then of a thick, frothy mucus, and later, perhaps, of blood. The animal shows pain upon pressure on the stomach just at the lower border of the last ribs, which is more or less severe according to the intensity of the inflammation.

If the cat is in freedom, and is able to get at fresh grass, it will itself eat a sufficient quantity to act as an emetic, which affords temporary relief. In the house-cat this can be replaced by a dose of a strong solution of Glauber's salts—a teaspoonful to a quarter-tumbler of water—of which several teaspoonsful can be given. This will act as an emetic, and a certain portion will be absorbed and act as a laxative. Should the vomiting continue, and there be much pain, give five to ten drops of paregoric, with two or three drops of extract of ginger, and a teaspoonful of a solution of gum arabic and water, and repeat every few hours.

Constipation and Diarrhœa.

Constipation is much less frequent in the cat than in other animals. On the contrary, there is a tendency in the cat, especially in the house-kept one, to a certain amount of looseness of the bowels, which would be looked on in other animals as suspicious. When this looseness becomes excessive, and the discharges become watery, or mixed with mucus, or even bloody, it takes the name of diarrhœa. When the diarrhœa becomes chronic, or is excessively severe, it takes the name of dysentery. In this case there is usually great straining, with very little discharge at each evacuation, and sometimes protrusion of the mucous membrane at the anus. Diarrhœa is frequently produced in the cat by feeding it out of soiled pans in which the milk or other food has been allowed to ferment. It is produced by irregular feeding—overfeeding the animal at one time and allowing it to starve at another. The use of fat meat, of putrid meat, and of too much liver or sour milk are also causes.

Jaundice — Yellows.

Jaundice, while it is the term frequently used to indicate a disease, is only a symptom of a disease, as evidenced by the yellow coloration of the mucous membrane of the eyes, and even, in severe cases, of the skin over the surface of the body and of the discharges. Jaundice is due to a disease of the liver, which may be either a temporary congestion or a chronic anatomical change in the structure of the liver, which in either case interferes with the function of this organ, and prevents its eliminating the bile, which is a waste product of the blood. This bile, then, not being carried off by its natural emunctory, must find some exit from the body, and is carried to the surface of the mucous membranes and skin, which are more important excretory glands for waste matter than they are usually given credit for. In case of congestion of the liver, examination of the right-hand side of the body, just under and behind the last ribs, will show a tumor or swelling, and a certain degree of tenderness, according to the acuteness of the congestion.

In case of chronic disease of the liver, hypertrophy or cirrhosis, the liver may be enlarged or diminished in size. The liver may also be affected with hydatids or other parasites, which produce similar symptoms.

In cases of constipation an examination should be made of the rectum, and a thorough examination of the abdomen should be made by manipulating the walls until the contents can be felt; for constipation in the cat is in the majority of cases due to a mechanical obstruction. I have at various times found this obstruction to be a bone which has been swallowed, bits of coal, pebbles, or a button which has been swallowed and acted as a nucleus for the accumulation of food around it, or balls of hair, called ægagropila, which have been made by the felting of the hair which the cat has licked off of its own sides. In one case the obstruction was a small fish-hook, which had passed through the entire length of the intestinal tract, and had lodged within an inch of the orifice of the anus. In this case I judged that the point of the hook had been protected during its first passage in a bit of hard fish-gill, which only had become absorbed, leaving the point free when it had nearly been passed. If any obstruction is found it should be removed, and the evacuation of the accumulated matter hastened by a dose of one or two tablespoonsful of castor-oil, or a somewhat larger quantity of syrup of buckthorn. The intestine of the cat is such a simple tube that by careful manipulation almost any obstruction can be worked down.

In case of diarrhœa the diet must be regulated from the outset. The animal can be given, at intervals of two hours, a powder made of one-eighth grain of calomel and five grains of saccharated pepsin. It should also be given small doses (thirty drops to one teaspoonful) of syrup of buckthorn, which, by stimulating the secretion from the surface of the intestine, relieves its congested condition. Should the diarrhœa be more severe, or become chronic, and be mixed with blood, tending to dysentery, or should the animal seem to be in much pain, as shown by its cries, and by tenderness upon pressure over the belly, give thirty-drop doses of paregoric, with teaspoonful doses of the mixture of chalk (*Mistura Creta*). This can be repeated every two, three, or four hours, according to the continued severity or the subsidence of the symptoms. In chronic cases, also, which tend to debilitate the animal, a half-teaspoonful dose of brandy can be added to the other treatment.

In jaundice the calomel must be used in one-tenth or one-twelfth grain doses, with a few grains of saccharated pepsin, given once every hour for a period of twelve or eighteen hours, and then followed by a full dose of castor-oil, or, perhaps preferably, by a purgative dose of sulphate of soda (thirty grains to one tablespoonful of water). Then for a day or two keep the animal on a moderate diet of milk, with a half-teaspoonful of bicarbonate of soda in each saucer of water; and at the end of that time the calomel can be repeated in the same doses, at an hour's interval each, for eight or ten hours.

Constitutional Diseases.

Distemper.

Distemper is a contagious and infectious fever of the cat, complicated by inflammations of the various organs of the body. Distemper is usually a disease of young cats, which, having once had it and having recovered, are protected from future attacks. It is, however, sometimes seen in older cats, especially so when the disease occurs in enzoötic or epizoötic form. Fleming, in his work upon "Sanitary Medicine," tells us that in the fifteenth century, and at several periods later, there were extensive epizoötics of distemper, which destroyed numbers of cats throughout central Europe and the British Islands. The last considerable epizoötic in England was in 1796. This extended also to the Low Countries, or the Netherlands. The same epizoötic extended to America in 1803.

The first symptoms of distemper are those of fever, with the combination of symptoms which are described above under Evidences of Disease. These may be more or less severe according to the gravity of the attack. Shortly after the commencement of the fever we find a watery discharge from the eyes, which may become mattery later; a discharge from the nostrils of a thick mucus at first, and matter later, which may even be tinged with blood. The disease may be followed later by any of the diseases of the respiratory system or of the digestive system, which in their local appearance are the same as those already described under diseases of these systems, but which are more severe than they are in their sporadic form, because they are grafted onto the body of an animal already suffering from fever and weakened by it.

Let it be understood, however, that in cases which have been going on for some little time, while the present condition of the animal is perfectly evident, it is not possible to make a diagnosis between these two following conditions:

1. A cat which has been infected first with distemper, has developed fever, and has the complication of a severe broncho-pneumonia or of a severe diarrhœa, or is excessively debilitated and weak; or

2. A cat which has been affected with a severe bronchitis and broncho-pneumonia, or a severe diarrhœa which is continued for some little time, and has produced by the local irritation and inflammation a fever which is secon-

dary, and from which the cat has been weakened and is greatly debilitated.

The conditions to be found upon physical examination in these two cases are absolutely identical, and the treatment for it is practically the same. Suppose, however, that not one cat alone, but several, are found in the same house or stable in the same condition, or in variable degrees pointing toward the same disease, or that we have from the owner a history that during the last few weeks, or for a longer or shorter period, other cats have been presenting the same symptoms, then we can assume it to be distemper.

Treatment of Distemper.—The cat with distemper must be isolated at once, and put into a quiet room where it is well protected from drafts of air, while still supplied with fresh air. It should be kept warm. At the outset, before the complications become marked, it can have a little bicarbonate of soda, or sulphur, in its water or milk, and a very light laxative. It should never be given an active cathartic, as this tends to excite diarrhœa. The catarrh, bronchitis, broncho-pneumonia, and diarrhœa which complicate distemper must be treated at the outset exactly as the same diseases would have been treated in their sporadic form. The strength of the animal must be kept up, but do not force food unless it is absolutely necessary. The local diseases complicating distemper require more stimulating treatment than they do in their simpler form, and the best stimulant is small doses of twenty to thirty drops of whisky or brandy.

Glanders.

It is not the place in a book of this sort to go into any extended description of glanders, as it is rarely found in cats other than in those around knackers' yards, in zoölogical gardens, or in the post-mortem rooms of a veterinary college; but practitioners should always bear in mind the susceptibility of the feline race to this disease. Glanders is a constitutional disease accompanied by the formation of tubercles over the mucous membrane of the respiratory tract and over the skin, which break down into ulcers, and of tubercles in the lungs themselves and in some of the other organs, which grow into small, hard, fibrous tumors. The ulcers in the nostrils or on the surface of the skin extend and destroy the tissues rapidly, producing an offensive discharge. The tubercles of the lungs cause broncho-pneumonia, which is usually fatal. Glanders, while a disease proper to the horse, is contagious to both man and the domestic cat, and all the rest of the cat tribe, as well as to other animals.

I have seen a number of lions die in a menagerie from having eaten glandered meat. In the post-mortem house of a veterinary college, in which I had just made an autopsy upon a glandered horse, as I was washing my hands I noticed a cat with a litter of kittens eating at some of the organs which I had placed to one side for demonstration. I had the cats immediately locked up, and in four days all of them were infected with the disease and had to be destroyed.

There is no treatment, and the animals must be immediately destroyed and the greatest precaution taken in regard to disinfection.

Eczema.

Eczema is the cutaneous manifestation of a constitutional trouble of a gouty nature. Eczema consists of a hyperemia of the skin, followed by exudation and desquamation of the cuticle. The symptoms are rough, dry hairs which become brittle and break off, an oily-appearing exudation around the roots of the hairs, and dry scabs which, as they peel off, leave little ulcerated surfaces. This eruption takes place principally along the line of the back and at the root of the tail, but in some more severe cases may extend to the sides of the body, legs, neck, and face. Eczema is sometimes called the "red mange," but is to be distinguished from the mange, which is a parasitic disease, the lesions of which appear on the under surface of the body and in the softer skin of the inside of the thighs.

Canker of the Ear.

Canker of the ear is one of the forms of eczema. It consists of a discharge, at first brownish, which may afterward become mattery, from the inside of the external ear. If this continues, the delicate skin lining the ear becomes ulcerated and excessively painful. The cat scratches at its ear in attempting to relieve the pain, and produces wounds on the ear itself, which from constant rubbing and irritation become chronic ulcers.

The cause of eczema is a lymphatic condition in the constitution of the animal. Certain families are more lymphatic than others, and they are predisposed to it. Constant confinement in the house, want of exercise, and over-feeding are the principal exciting causes.

We also have, however, another form of eczema which is due to want of nutrition. This we sometimes find in young, half-grown kittens, or cats which have been badly nourished or almost starved.

The treatment of eczema is based, first, essentially, upon a strict attention to diet and régime. An over-fed cat must be starved — a poorly fed cat must be properly nourished. Diuretics and laxatives in the form of five-grain doses of Rochelle salts or Glauber's salts, and one-grain doses of iodide of potash can be combined with tonics. The best of the latter are quinine, Huxham's tincture, and syrup of wild cherry bark. Fowler's solution may be used in two-drop doses. Baths of sulphur water are beneficial. If there is much irritation an ointment of one part bitrine ointment and eight parts of lard is soothing and healing. In canker of the ear, iodoform as a powder, or mixed with balsam of Peru, can be dropped into the ear. Once a day the ear should be cleansed with a pleget of cotton on a match or small probe.

Milk-fever.

When an entire litter of kittens has been removed from the mother at once, the accumulation of milk swells the mammary glands, and, if not relieved, cakes, and produces a local inflammation in this organ, which ends with the formation of abscesses, and is excessively painful. The irritation of this *mammitis*, as the local trouble is called, produces a considerable amount of fever, attended with vomiting and sometimes diarrhœa. A wound or other injury to the mammary glands of a cat who is nursing her young may produce the same disease.

Milk-fever is to be treated with the ordinary remedies for fever, and a local application to the mammary glands of belladona ointment, alone, or mixed with mercurial ointment.

Nervous Troubles.

Convulsions or Fits.

Convulsions or fits in the cat occur occasionally. The symptoms vary considerably according to the period of the convulsion in which the animal is seen, and according to the severity of the attack. At the outset the animal becomes excited, runs, jumps, and if caught, struggles to escape without using any special judgment or volition. It may froth at the mouth, the legs become rigid, or the muscles contract and become relaxed alternately in quick spasms. Following this comes a period of depression, in which the animal may lie in a state of coma, absolutely senseless and apparently dead. From this condition it may awake to a renewed attack of spasm, or it may gradually sleep it off, and be apparently perfectly well, except somewhat weakened and depressed for a short period. Convulsions in cats are far more frequent in young animals than in old, and are usually due to digestive irritation—either that of overfeeding or of the ingestion of irritating food. In summertime they are often the result of heat, perhaps also at other times from the same cause; but I myself doubt if heat alone is frequently a cause, unless combined with an overloaded stomach.

Epilepsy.

In epilepsy, with few premonitory symptoms, unless it be a single scream, the cat falls to the ground, its mouth frothing, its eyes rolling in the sockets until the whites show, the legs stretching in spasms, with moments of temporary relaxation, and then a complete subsidence of the symptoms, when the animal falls to sleep to wake up apparently unharmed. If the cat has frequent attacks it becomes very much debilitated and loses its vivacity. The diagnosis of epileptic attacks from those of ordinary convulsions is based upon the absence of delirium and the presence of the pivoting eyeballs in epilepsy. Sometimes in epilepsy the cat may bite its tongue or injure its lips against the ground in its struggles, when we have a mixture of blood with the froth in the mouth.

The first thing to do for a cat in convulsions is to prevent foolish meddlers from scaring it to death. Wrap it up at once in a soft cloth so that it cannot injure itself. A small dose of chloral or laudanum may be useful to quiet the attack, but combine this with a full dose of castor-oil or syrup of buckthorn. Bleeding at the ear, cold water over the head and body, and such measures have been recommended, but I prefer a warm, soft blanket.

Parasitic Diseases.

Fleas (P. serraticeps).

Fleas are not nearly as common on cats as they are credited with being. The flea on the cat is not the same one which affects people, and if transferred to man, does not remain. They can be readily got rid of by sprinkling the cat's basket, or its back, with flowers of sulphur, Persian insect-powder, or powdered tobacco, which can then be well brushed out; or the cat can be sponged over

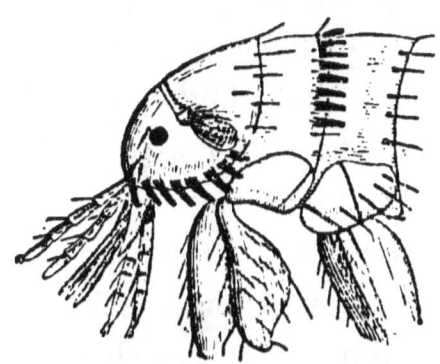

Fig. 22.—Pulex Serraticeps.
(*Enlarged* 30 *diameters.*)

with a five-percent. solution of carbolic acid. Persian insect-powder, however, is the preferable treatment. In using it, place the cat on a large newspaper, and after brushing the powder out, burn the paper and contents, as the flea is not killed—only stunned for the moment.

Mange (*Sarcoptus notoedres*, var. *Cati*).

The ordinary mange, or sarcoptic mange, is due to a small parasite which burrows under the skin, where it deposits its eggs, which, upon hatching, become very irritating to the skin, as the young insects grow and tunnel out to the surface, where they breed, for the next generation again to burrow and deposit its eggs. The sarcoptic mange may appear first on the face and sides of the cheek, or upon the insides of the armpits and thighs; and it gradually extends over the softer skin of the inside of the thighs, the under surface of the belly, and even, in extreme cases, over almost the entire body. The itchiness produced by the mange causes the animal to scratch and rub itself, which further irritates the skin, producing abrasions which scab over; and as the scabs are in turn scratched off, they leave irritating, bleeding, and ugly ulcers. In severe cases the constant irritation and worry to the animal cause it to lose its appetite, and it may become excessively debilitated and emaciated. The cause and effect then become retroactive, as the mange will extend more rapidly on a debilitated animal, and the increase of the mange increases the debility.

There are a great many remedies for the mange, and it is not so much the choice of the remedy to be used as the manner of its application which is efficacious. One of the simplest modes of treatment is sulphur ointment. One dram of flowers of sulphur to the ounce of pure lard should be well rubbed into the skin

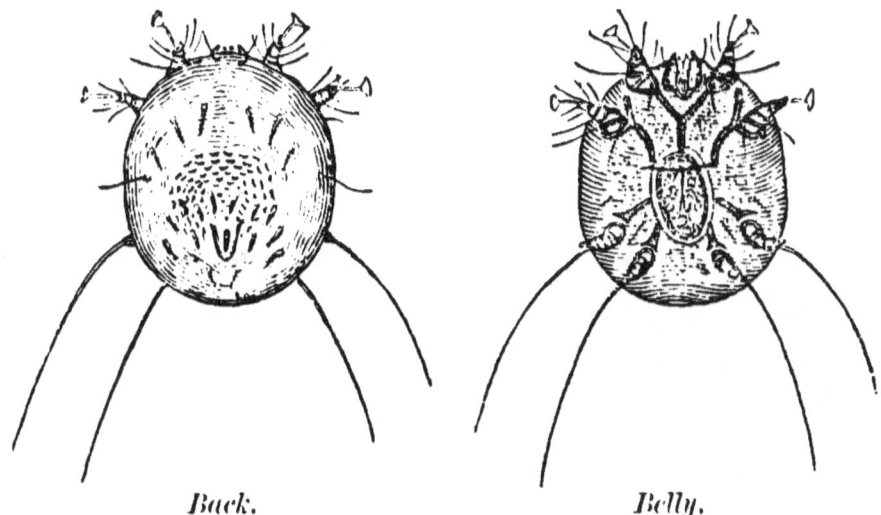

Back.   Belly.

FIG. 23.—SARCOPTUS CATI (FEMALE).

and all parts affected, and repeated for several days in succession. The skin should then be well sponged off with a little soap and tepid water, and allowed to remain clean for a day or two. The body should then be well brushed with a moderately stiff brush, which will remove any scabs on the skin, when the ointment is to be reapplied for several days. A mixture of one part of coal-tar, one part of oil of cade, and six or eight parts of benzine is an excellent remedy, although less cleanly. It should be applied with a moderately stiff brush daily for four days in succession, when the animal should be sponged off with tepid water and soap, and at the end of two days the application renewed. If the animal is much debilitated it can be put on a tonic treatment of one grain of quinine in thirty drops of whisky three times in the day, or upon teaspoonful doses of a mixture of equal parts of syrup of wild-cherry bark and Huxham's tincture. Two-drop doses of Fowler's solution, given three times a day on a little piece of cake, bread, or anything which the cat will take from the hand, is an excellent tonic.

Follicular Mange (Demodex folliculorum).

Follicular mange, which is due to a parasite called the *Demodex folliculorum*, affects the nose around the muzzle, the skin of the chin, and the skin of the paws surrounding the claws, where it burrows in beside the roots of the whiskers and larger and grosser hairs, and

DISEASES OF CATS 115

into the sebaceous glands. This insect is extremely irritating, causing the animal to rub and scratch. Examination around the roots of the whiskers and on the skin of the paws

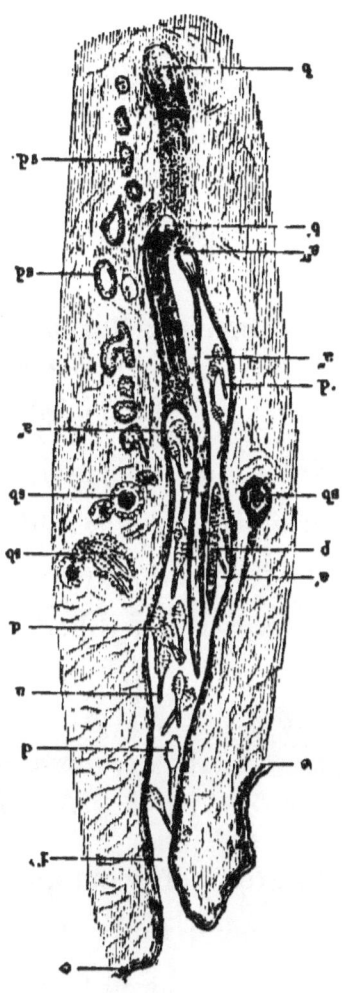

Fig. 24.—Hair-follicle and Sebaceous Glands Affected by Demodex Folliculorum.

will show dark-red pimples or pustules about the size of a pinhead. This form of mange is sometimes difficult to get rid of. It can be treated with the preparation of coal-tar and

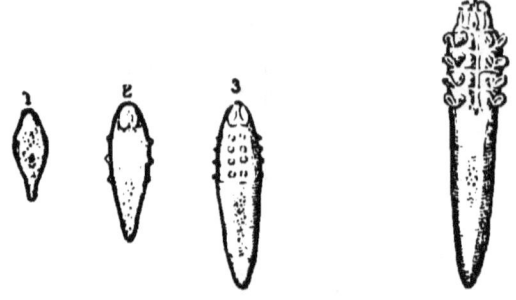

Fig. 25.—Demodex Folliculorum.
(*Enlarged* 100 *Diameters.*)
1, The egg; 2, Larva hexapod; 3, Larva octopod.

oil of cade given above, which must be well rubbed in with a stiff brush, and which can be alternated every four days by an application of mercurial ointment well rubbed into the same parts.

Stomach-worms (*Ascarides of the Cat*).
(*A. mystax*, Zeder; *A. felis*, Gmelin.)

The so-called stomach-worm, which is found both in the stomach and in the intestines, especially of young cats, is a worm from two to three or four inches in length, about the size of small slate-pencils, pointed at the ends, which are somewhat curved. The tail has two small membranous wings, with twenty-six papillæ on each side, of which five are post-anal. The female is somewhat longer than the

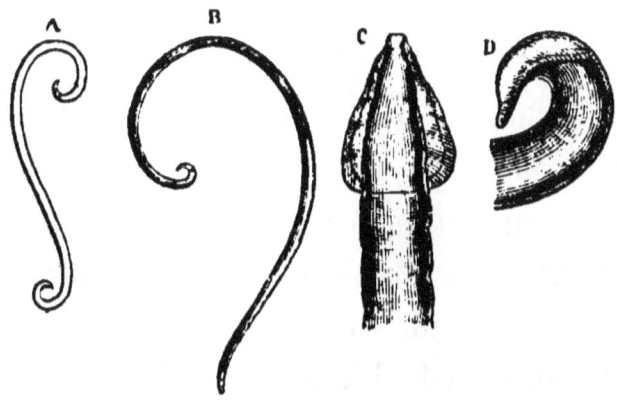

FIG. 26.—ASCARIS MYSTAX.
a, Male; *b*, Female; *c*, Anterior extremity; *d*, Seen in profile.

male. This species of ascarides inhabits not only the intestines of the cat, but those of a large number of the savage species of the genus *Felis*.

The symptoms of the presence of this worm are only those of intestinal irritation; and even these may not be present, and the diagnosis can then only be made by seeing one of the worms which has been passed. The treatment consists of diet for twenty-four hours, then a good purgative dose of castor-oil. This may be preceded by half an hour by a three-grain dose of santonin, and in large cats five drops of turpentine may be added to the oil.

Tapeworm (*Tænia crassicolis*).

The whole of the feline tribe is a frequent host of the tapeworm, of which it has a variety of its own (*Tænia crassicolis*). The worm is from six to twenty-four inches in length. It has a large head, set on a narrow neck. The head is provided with a crown of from twenty-six to fifty-two hooks—frequently only thirty-four in number. The body is made up of a series of segments or rings, as can be seen in the illustration (Figure 27). The tapeworm inhabits the small intestine of the cat, the head remaining fastened to the mucous membrane of the intestine, while the body floats off in the soft contents. The end of the tail, or various portions of the body, break away from time to time, to be carried to the exterior to develop into fresh foci of infection. As the body breaks away from the tail, it keeps growing from the head. In its vesicular form the tapeworm is

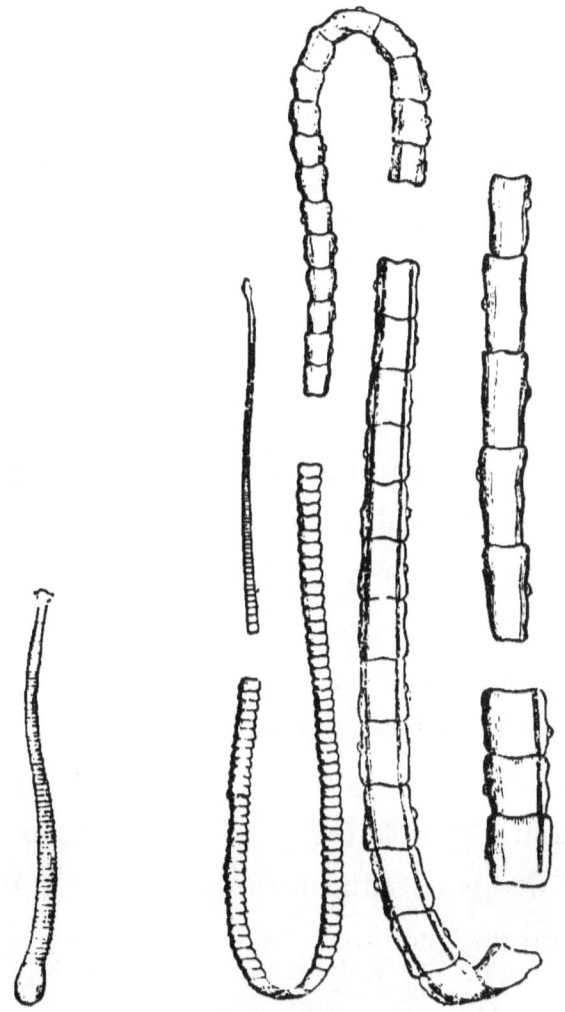

Fig. 27.—Tænia Crassicollis.

found in the livers of rats and mice, which, when they are eaten by the cat, again infect it. The tapeworm, unless existing in quantities, causes little irritation. What symptoms do exist are those of intestinal irritation — occasional bloating or swelling up of the belly of the animal, and sometimes emaciation. The diagnosis can only be accurately made by recognizing the segments of the worm which are carried away with the fæces, and which appear as small oblong whitish masses, sometimes single or sometimes connected together.

The treatment consists of putting the cat upon an absolute diet for twenty-four hours; then give, according to the size of the animal, from ten to twenty grains of powdered areca and two to four grains of santonin. This can readily be given in a saucer of milk, which the animal willingly swallows, having been starved for a day. The powder is to be followed in two hours by a full dose of castor-oil, to which a few drops of turpentine or a few grains of jalap might be added.

Ringworm (Tinea tonsurans).

Ringworm in the cat appears in the form of little round spots from the size of a ten-cent piece to the size of a quarter-dollar. Sometimes the various spots run into each other and form irregular-shaped spots, the edges of which, however, always assume the rounded form. In these spots the hairs are broken off, leaving little bristling points only protruding from the roots. The surface of the skin itself is covered by a furfuraceous scab, which, if peeled or rubbed off, shows a slight exudation below. If not attended to, the disease keeps spreading to new parts of the body as fast as the older spots heal. Ringworm is due to a vegetable parasite known as *Trichophyton tonsurans*. The cat is probably one of the most common sources of the propagation of this disease to the human being, especially children. The cat in turn probably, in the majority of cases, contracts the disease, not from others of its own kind, but from sewer-rats which are caught as prey.

Some years ago, while I had charge of the dispensary of the Children's Hospital at Philadelphia, I collected a large number of statistics in regard to the children who came to the hospital with ringworm. They, of course, represented the poorer classes. Invariably I found that the patients had in the house a cat which they played with; and I verified the origin by examining their cats and finding them affected with the disease. A cat with ringworm should be isolated for a few days from the children and from other cats, until the spots have been well rubbed with mercurial ointment for several days in succession. Then the animal should be watched daily for the next week or two for the appearance of fresh spots, which should be treated with mercurial ointment the instant they appear.

Trichina (*Trichina spiralis*).

Trichina is not a rare parasite in the cat, but its diagnosis is excessively difficult. The *Trichina spiralis*, in its vesicular form, is found in the rat and in the hog, the flesh of both of which animals, of course, is common food for the cat. When eaten, the parasite wakens into life, develops into the little worm which is seen in the figure (Figure 28), and mixes with the contents of the stomach and intestines. Fortunately these frequently develop irritation, which produces a diarrhœa in the animal, and the majority of them are carried off. But in other cases some of the worms pierce the intestines and travel into the muscles of the body.

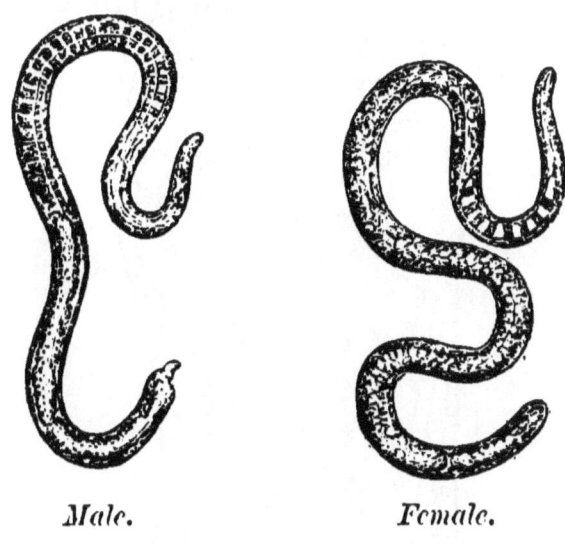

Male. Female.
Fig. 28.—Trichina Spiralis.

If they exist in small numbers, appreciable symptoms are not visible. If, however, they invade the muscles in large quantities, they produce pains which resemble greatly those of rheumatism, and they may produce a fever lasting for a few days. The invasion, if excessive, may produce death. In other cases the worm becomes encysted in the cat's muscles (Figure 29), and produces no after-effect. The diagnosis can only be made by a recognition of

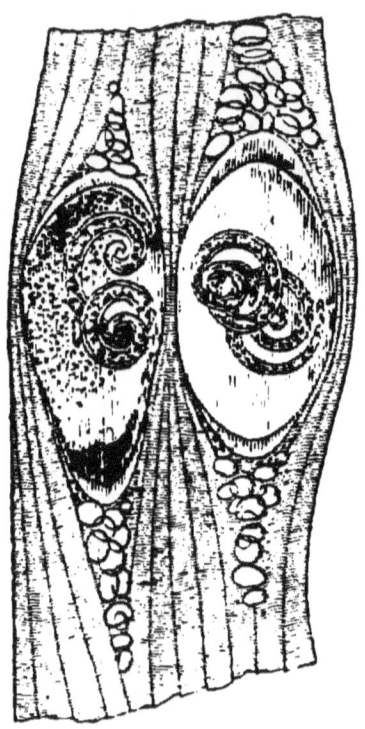

Fig. 29.—Trichinæ Encysted in Muscular Tissue.

the parasite. In the human being suspected cases of trichina-poisoning have been verified by harpooning small bits of muscles from the sore arm or leg of the patient, and demonstrating the presence of the parasite by the microscope.

Cause of Parasitic Broncho-pneumonia.
(*Vide page 92.*)

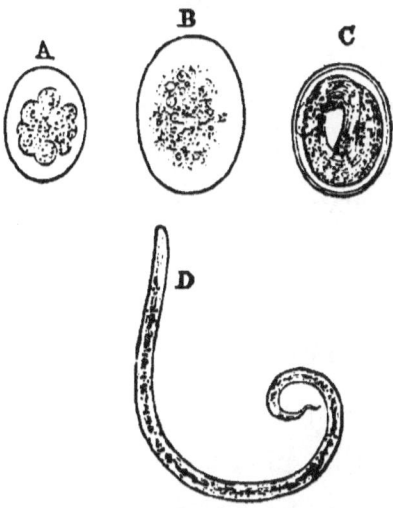

FIG. 30.—STRONGYLUS PULMONIS.
a, b, Eggs segmenting; *c*, Egg with embryo; *d*, Embryo free.

THE EYES.

In all fevers, distemper, and other grave troubles, the eyes of the cat become congested and water somewhat, or become filled with a mucous or mattery discharge which glues the lids together. If this becomes excessive or chronic there may be an inflammation of the conjunctiva—the mucous membrane lining the eyelids and covering the eyes—which produces raw lids. In any simple trouble of the eyes they should be well washed with tepid water or tepid water and milk, and have a few drops of a solution of one-half grain of the sulphate of atropia, one and a half grains of the sulphate of zinc, and one ounce of rose-water put in them several times a day.

From an excessive conjunctivitis, or from injury from a scratch or blow on the eyeball itself, we may have an inflammation of the cornea, which clouds the eye over with a large white spot (*keratitis*). This, if attended to at once, is usually not serious, although it may be followed by ulceration of the cornea, which allows the escape of the humor of the eye.

Cataract, or inflammation of the crystalline lens of the eyes, followed later by a deposit of calcareous matter in the lens, sometimes occurs. In this case the front of the eye is entirely clear, while a frozen, snowlike mass can be seen through the pupil, which is chronically dilated.

Wounds and traumatisms to the eyelids and the eye itself present the same symptoms and require the same treatment that similar injuries would in other animals.

The Teeth.

As we have seen before, the young cat has twenty-six teeth, which it changes at about six months of age for thirty permanent ones. This change of teeth is frequently attended by considerable irritation of the gums, and pain, which interferes with the animal's eating, and may cause some little fever or produce a slight diarrhœa. It also gives the breath of the animal an offensive odor. The mouth should be examined, and any teeth which are loosened should be picked out with a pair of forceps, and the mouth sponged out with some listerine, which can be done by tying a small sponge on the end of a stick, or by using a large camel's-hair brush.

In old cats, as the teeth become worn, and especially in cats which are constantly fed with soft food and do not have an opportunity of rubbing their teeth clean by catching natural prey or using them on hard substances, there occurs a deposit of tartar around the roots of the teeth, which causes ulceration of the gums, and sometimes necrosis of the jaw-bone itself.

This is very painful, interferes with the animal's eating, and produces an offensive odor. The mouth should be very carefully examined; any loosened teeth should be pulled, and the others should be cleaned with a small scraper. The gums should then be well washed with listerine. Such a mouth cannot be cured rapidly, but requires attention every week or two for some little time.

The Claws.

The claws of the cat are, as we have seen, protected, when not required for use, by being drawn back into the sockets, which are peculiar to this class of animals. This protection keeps the points of the claws perfectly sharp for catching their prey; for if they protruded as they do in the dog, they would become worn off and be as dull as those of the latter. The claws sometimes get injured by being broken when seizing rough objects, or from accidents, which renders them excessively sore. If the nail only has been loosened, it should be trimmed off carefully, and a little balsam applied to the uncovered bone, which will soon grow a new claw. If, however, the bone has been injured, and has become necrosed, it should be removed. In injuries of this sort, when the bone is affected, the sooner it is attended to the better. If only the extremity of the bone is diseased, it can be scraped off, and will heal rapidly; whereas if the necrosis has extended to the joint, and has implicated the elastic ligament, healing is difficult, and amputation may have to be performed as high as the second joint.

POISONS.

Cats are subject to mineral poisons given them intentionally, or left carelessly lying in corners mixed with food intended for rats, which the cat gets at accidentally. The usual mineral poisons are arsenic or rat-poison. The cat may also be poisoned from verdigris and salts of copper, which form on the surface of improperly cleaned kitchen-utensils left with food standing in them, which the cats eat. Mineral poisons produce irritation of the stomach, violent pain, vomiting, and, if they do not prove fatal, diarrhœa at a later time. Fortunately they do usually produce vomiting, so that the animal gets rid of the excess of poison; and this indicates the treatment, which should be at once an active emetic, consisting of one-half teaspoonful of mustard in a little warm water, or a saturated solution of Glauber's salts in warm water, given in as large quantity as possible, and repeated until violent vomiting is produced. The after-treatment, if the animal is left debilitated, consists of stimulants, with the white of an egg, or a solution of starch, to allay the irritation.

Strychnine poisoning frequently occurs from the same intention or accident by which cats are poisoned with mineral poisons. The symptoms of strychnine poisoning are a characteristic spasm. The cat gives a cry or two, and lies stretched out, with the head and neck thrown back, the hind legs extended rigidly, and the forelegs drawn down by the side of the body. Cases of strychnine poisoning, if recognized at once and treated immediately with large doses of chloral hydrate—especially if the latter can be given by injection with a hypodermic syringe—in a large number of cases can be saved. The chloral can be given in poisonous diseases as high as ten or twenty grains or more the first dose, and ten grains every half-hour.

ADMINISTRATION OF MEDICINE.

In well-broken cats fond of their owner the administration of medicine is sometimes an easy matter; but again in equally well-broken and affectionate animals it is an excessively difficult matter.

In pill or powder form the substance used can sometimes be inclosed in a small piece of meat or other food, which the animal will readily swallow. Again, however, the cat becomes excessively suspicious of the faintest odor of medicine, and after taking it once or twice will refuse it. Liquid medicine—which should never exceed a teaspoonful dose if it can be helped—must be poured into the mouth. At the outset it can be tried if the cat will take its medicine without contention. Place the cat on a table, pat it gently until, with one hand, the head can be grasped from behind so that the thumb covers the jaw on one side, the second finger the jaw on the other side, and the first finger lies on top of the head between the ears. The third finger of the hand covers the jaw underneath. The head should then be gently raised, the thumb and second finger draw the commissures of the lips gently backward until they make a pocket on one or the other side, into which the liquid can be poured. It is not necessary to open the jaw itself, as the liquid will run through the teeth.

In many cases, however, more stringent measures are required, and the cat must be held so that it cannot bite or scratch. The simplest method, which is all that is required in some cases, and for the operation of castration, is to have an attendant take the cat by the loose skin of the neck and over the shoulders with one hand, and by the skin from the pelvis or croup with the other hand. Then place it upon a table and press down until the breast-bone in front and the under surface of the pelvis behind are held firmly against the table. It is then impossible for the cat to use either its fore or hind legs to scratch, or for it to twist its head to bite, and the second person can examine the mouth and administer medicine or operate. Absolute care must be taken, however, that no pressure is put upon the ribs, or the chest itself, or upon the belly of the animal, as carelessness in this point may stop the respiration and prove fatal. If more complete contention is required—as it is for operations which last for any length of time, or for any very obstreperous animals—the cat should be wrapped in a sack of cloth or soft leather, or of india-rubber. Where a large number of cats are handled, it is well to have a sheet of leather such as a blacksmith uses for his apron, with a whole in the centre just large enough to admit the head of the cat. This is drawn over the head, and the corners of the leather are carefully folded along the line of the body into an oblong sack, which must be firmly held. Care must be taken to draw the forelegs backward along the side of the body, and hold them so, firmly, as the neck of the cat is smaller than its head, and after being drawn over the head the hole in the leather will admit of the protrusion of the cat's forelegs, and the animals are great adepts at getting the forelegs out unless especial care is taken.

ANESTHETICS.

Anesthetics, especially in the shape of chloroform and of ether, are frequently advised for operations on cats. Unless absolute immobility of the animal is required for the success of the operation, I do not like the use of anesthetics. To begin with, even carefully given, they are dangerous. I have found that animals to which I have given an anesthetic are more afraid of me afterward than those which I have simply had held properly and produced pain upon. The pain they understand as done for their good; the use of the anesthetics they do not understand. For many operations, however, it is perfectly permissible to use a preliminary injection of cocaine, which annuls the pain in a local part.

DESTROYING CATS.

We are unfortunately frequently obliged to destroy cats for economic reasons, or for humane reasons, to prevent suffering in animals which cannot get well. In large institutions, like the Home of the American Society for the Prevention of Cruelty to Animals, they have tanks containing carbonic acid, which puts the animal to sleep and death painlessly. Drowning is an equally quick and painless death, if done properly; but care must be taken that the animal is quickly and totally immersed in water, and not allowed to reach the surface for a single instant for a gasp of air. By this method, undoubtedly, the animal has one momentary shock, and an attempted gasp, when formation of carbonic acid in its own brain puts it to sleep and renders it unconscious before even death takes place.

Poisoning by strychnine or arsenic is cruel, as it produces considerable pain before death. Strong prussic acid generally produces immediate death; but it is difficult to administer, and in some cases it fails absolutely.

In the hands of an expert, while it has the appearance of brutality, a ball from a pistol, or a properly administered blow with a hammer on the skull, produces instantaneous and painless death; but these methods should not be adopted by any one whose experience does not warrant him in doing it properly, completely, and at the first attempt.

Chloroform in the hands of a novice is perhaps the simplest method, if he use the following precautions:

Take a box or large pail with a cover which can be firmly closed; use plenty of chloroform (at least two to four ounces); place the cat in the receptacle; pour the chloroform on a sponge, and drop it in beside the cat; place the cover on and hold firmly in place for some time. In this way the only annoyance to the cat is probably its first moment of fright, and the single gasp or two which it makes for fresh air before the chloroform has commenced to act.

CHAPTER VI.

ETYMOLOGY AND SYNONYMS.

THE word "cat" comes from a root of unknown origin; but undoubtedly it is almost identical with the original Aryan word which was used for this animal, as we find a close similarity throughout all the Aryan languages in the euphony and terseness of the word.

English, *cat*.
   Grimalkin, an old cat, especially a she-cat.
   Pussy, a pet name for the cat. (The word "puss" indicates a hare, as well as a cat.)
Anglo-Saxon, *cat*.
Old Anglo-Saxon, *catt*.
Danish, *kat*.
Swedish, *katt*.
Icelandic, *köttr*.
Irish, *cat*.
Welsh, *cath*.

German, *katze, kater.*
Old German, *chazza.*
Latin, *catus.*
French, *chat.*
Italian, *gatto,* feminine *gatta.*
Spanish, *gato.*
Greek, κάττα.
New Greek, γάττα.
Russian and Polish, *kot.*
Armenian, *kaz.*
Turkish, *kedi.*
Arabic, *qitt.*

EMBLEMATIC SIGNIFICATION OF THE CAT.

The figure of the cat has certain significations when reproduced in art.

In the hieroglyphics of the ancient monuments of Egypt a cat represents false friendship, or a deceitful, flattering friend.

In heraldry a cat is an emblem of liberty, because it naturally dislikes to be shut up; and therefore the Burgundians, etc., bore a cat on their banners to intimate that they could not endure servitude.

It is a bold and daring creature, and also cruel to its enemy, and never gives over till it has destroyed it, if possible. It is also watchful, dexterous, swift, pliable, and has good nerves—thus, if it falls from a place never so high, it still alights on its feet—and therefore may denote those who have such forethought that whatsoever befalls them they are still on their guard.

In coat-armor the cat must always be represented as full-faced, and not showing one side of it, but both its eyes and both its ears. *Argent* three cats in pale *sable* is the coat of the family of Keat of Devonshire.

In recent years it has become the emblematic animal of newspaper offices and the editor's chair.

APPENDIX.

I HAVE appended (Table A) a reduced form of entry as used by the National Cat Show, and (Table B) a classification of the divisions which they make of the various cats. It will be seen that there is, first, a distinct division into the Long-haired Cats and the Short-haired Cats; second, that there are four divisions into He-cats, She-cats, Gelded Cats, and Kittens. This, it will be seen, gives eight general divisions — Long-haired Cats divided according to sex and age, four; and Short-haired Cats divided according to sex and age, four. The third division is made by color, which consists of two classes of Tortoise-shell, one with and one without white; three classes of Tabbies divided according to the base color; Black-and-White Cats; cats of a solid color; and one class for cats of a color not defined in the preceding. Care must be taken that a cat is entered in its own proper class, because any carelessness in entering disqualifies a cat absolutely in that class, although it may be a magnificent animal, and if placed in its own class would easily win.

In Table C are given the Comparative Points of Judging recommended by Mr. John Jennings, which table is too extended for use except by an expert; but it readily shows the important points of value to be attached to the various parts. It will be seen that, to begin with, the length of the fur, the quality of the fur, and the frill, or those wavy crests of hair at points of juncture where the fur lies in opposite directions, are most important; second, that the color of the coat (which means the richness and purity of its coloring) and the tail (which includes size and carriage) are given about equal importance. The eyes, again, are given considerable importance, especially in the White and Self-colored Cats.

Table D gives the very excellent statute of the State of New York, which was procured by the efforts of the Society for the Prevention of Cruelty to Animals, and which has placed the care of animals under the control of the society. This has done away with the abominable and brutal muzzles which the law previously required for dogs, and has made owners much more careful in registering their dogs, and in not countenancing waifs in dogs or cats, which are always subject to careless inattention or positive cruelty. As we go to press, a bill has just passed the Assembly at Albany extending the provisions of this statute to the city of Brooklyn, and has also extended the powers of the society.

TABLE A.—ENTRY FORM.

To be filled up and sent with Entrance Fees to the Secretary of the NATIONAL CAT SHOW, Executive Office, Madison Square Garden, 26th Street, New York, not later than April 24th, 1895.

The Entrance Fee for each cat or pair of kittens is $1.00, and except for special prizes cats and pairs of kittens can be entered in one class only. Exhibitors must be careful to enter their cats in their proper classes and give their proper description as to color, sex, etc.

Class No.	Name of Cat.	Color and Description.	Sex.	Age.		If for sale, state Price, including Basket, Box, or Hamper.
				Years.	Months.	
						$

I hereby enter the above cats at my own Risk, and subject to the Rules and Regulations of the Show. Herewith I inclose $......Amount of Entrance Fees. Cheques or Money Orders to be made payable to the order of the Secretary of the National Cat Show.

PLEASE WRITE DISTINCTLY
AND STATE WHETHER MR., MRS., OR MISS. { Name.......... Address..........

N. B.—ENTRIES CLOSE WEDNESDAY, APRIL 24th.

TABLE B.

CLASSIFICATION OF CATS AT THE NATIONAL CAT SHOW.

BY SUB-ORDER.	BY SEX AND AGE.	BY BREED OR VARIETY.
I. Long-haired, Asiatic or Eastern cats (Persians, Angoras, Russians).	I. He-cats.	TORTOISE-SHELL. Color to be red, yellow, and black; no white.
		TORTOISE-SHELL-AND-WHITE. Color to be red, yellow, black, and white.
	II. She-cats.	BROWN OR DARK GRAY TABBY. Color to be rich brown or dark gray, striped or spotted with black; no white.
		SILVER OR BLUE TABBY. Color to be silver gray or blue, striped or spotted with black; no white.
II. Short-haired, European or Western Cats (Ordinary European Cats).	III. Gelded cats.	RED TABBY OR RED TABBY AND WHITE. Color to be reddish or sandy, striped or spotted with darker sandy and white.
		BLACK OR WHITE. Color to be entirely black or entirely white (Maltese). Blue or silver solid color, without white (Maltese).
	IV. Kittens over three months and under six months of age.	ANY OTHER VARIETY. Color to be any hue not specified in the foregoing classes. Manx cats, any color or sex.

TABLE C.

COMPARATIVE POINTS.—VALUE OF LONG-HAIRED CATS.

VARIETY.	Length of Fur.	Quality of Fur.	Frill.	Tail.	Color.	Markings.	Head.	Eyes.	Size.	Condition.	Total.
Any Self-color except White	20	16	12	12	12	—	5	8	5	10	100
White	20	15	12	12	10	—	5	10	6	10	100
Tabbies, any Color	15	10	10	10	15	15	5	5	5	10	100

COMPARATIVE POINTS.—VALUE OF SHORT-HAIRED CATS.

VARIETY.	Color.	Markings.	Size and Shape.	Quality of Fur.	Head.	Eyes.	Tail.	Condition.	Total.
Tortoise-shell	30	20	10	10	5	5	10	10	100
Self-colors { Black	30	—	20	15	10	10	5	10	100
Self-colors { White	25	—	15	20	10	15	5	10	100
Self-colors { Blue	35	—	15	20	10	5	5	10	100
Self-colors { Any other Color	25	—	15	25	10	10	5	10	100
Tortoise-shell-and-White	30	20	10	10	5	5	10	10	100
Silver Tabby	25	25	10	10	5	5	10	10	100
Red Tabby	30	20	15	10	5	5	5	10	100
Brown or other Striped Tabby	30	20	15	10	5	5	5	10	100
Spotted Tabby	25	30	10	10	5	5	5	10	100
Any Variety or Color, White Markings	20	30	15	10	5	5	5	10	100

COMPARATIVE POINTS.—VALUE OF OTHER DISTINCT VARIETIES.

MANX.

VARIETY.	Tailless.	Color.	Size and Shape Throughout.	Fur.	Markings.	Head.	Eyes.	Condition.	Total.
Self-color	30	20	20	10	—	5	5	10	100
With Markings	30	10	20	10	10	5	5	10	100

TABLE D.

LAWS 1894, CHAPTER 115.

Approved by the Governor, March 8, 1894.

An Act for the Better Protection of Lost and Strayed Animals, and for Securing the Rights of the Owners Thereof.

The People of the State of New York, represented in Senate and Assembly, do enact as follows:

Section 1. Every person who owns or harbors one or more dogs within the corporate limits of any city having a population of over twelve hundred thousand shall procure a yearly license for each animal, paying the sum of two dollars for each one, as hereinafter provided.

Sec. 2. Licenses granted under this act shall date from the first day of May in each year, and may be renewed at the expiration of the term by payment of one dollar for each renewal.

Sec. 3. Each certificate of license or renewal shall state the name and address of the owner of the dog, and also the number of such license or renewal.

Sec. 4. Every dog so licensed shall at all times have a collar about its neck, with a metal tag attached thereto bearing the number of the license stamped thereon.

Sec. 5. Dogs not licensed pursuant to the provisions of this act shall be seized, and if not redeemed within forty-eight hours may be destroyed or otherwise disposed of, as hereinafter provided.

Sec. 6. It is further provided that any cat found within the corporate limits of any such city without a collar about its neck bearing the name and residence of the owner stamped thereon may be seized and disposed of in like manner as prescribed above for dogs.

Sec. 7. Any person claiming a dog or cat seized under the provisions of this act, and proving ownership thereof, shall be entitled to resume possession of the animal on payment of the sum of three dollars.

Sec. 8. The American Society for the Prevention of Cruelty to Animals is hereby empowered and authorized to carry out the provisions of this act, and the said society is further authorized to issue licenses and renewals, and to collect the fees for such, as is herein prescribed, which fees are to be used by said society toward defraying the cost of carrying out the provisions of this act and maintaining a shelter for lost, strayed, or homeless animals.

Sec. 9. Any person or persons who shall hinder, molest, or interfere with any officer or agent of said society while in the performance of any duty enjoined by this act shall be deemed guilty of a misdemeanor, and upon conviction shall pay a fine of not less than twenty-five dollars nor more than one hundred dollars, or be imprisoned for not less than ten days nor more than thirty days, or be punished by both fine and imprisonment.

Sec. 10. None of the provisions of this act shall apply to dogs owned by non-residents passing through the city, nor to dogs brought to the city and entered for exhibition at any dog show.

Sec. 11. The thirtieth subdivision of section eighty-six of chapter four hundred and ten of the laws of eighteen hundred and eighty-two, entitled "An act to consolidate into one act and to declare the special and local laws affecting public interests in the city of New York," and all other acts and parts of acts inconsistent with the provisions of this act, are hereby repealed.

Sec. 12. This act shall take effect immediately.

THE END.

www.ingramcontent.com/pod-product-compliance
Lightning Source LLC
Chambersburg PA
CBHW030304170426
43202CB00009B/870